Guiding Tho　　 －　　 In Ohio

2nd Edition

LEGAL AND PRACTICAL THINGS
YOU NEED TO DO
TO SETTLE AN ESTATE IN OHIO

and

HOW TO ARRANGE YOUR OWN AFFAIRS
TO AVOID UNNECESSARY COSTS
TO YOUR FAMILY

By AMELIA E. POHL, ESQ.

and Ohio Attorney
MICHAEL JOSEPH O'BRIEN

 EAGLE PUBLISHING COMPANY OF BOCA

The purpose of this book is to provide the reader with an informative overview of the subject; but laws change frequently and are subject to different interpretations as courts rule on the meaning or effect of a law. This book is sold with the understanding that neither the authors, nor the editors, nor the publisher, nor the distributors of this book are engaging in, or rendering, legal, accounting, financial planning, or any other professional service. Pursuant to Internal Revenue Service guidance, be advised that any federal tax advice in this publication was not intended or written to be used, and it cannot be used, by any person or entity for the purpose of avoiding penalties imposed under the Internal Revenue Code (IRS Circular 230 Disclaimer). If you need legal, accounting, financial planning or any other expert advice, you should seek the services of a licensed professional.

This book is intended for use by the consumer for his or her own benefit. If you use this book to counsel someone about the law or tax matters, that may be considered to be an unlicensed and illegal practice. Web sites, telephone numbers and addresses appear throughout the book for the convenience of the reader; however, this information is subject to change as agencies move. Publication of a Web site is not an endorsement of that site by the authors, editors or publishers of this book.

EAGLE PUBLISHING COMPANY OF BOCA
4199 N. Dixie Highway, #2
Boca Raton, FL 33431   E-mail: info@eaglepublishing.com

Printed in the United State   ISBN 1-932464-19-0
Library of Congress Catalog Card Number: 00-190218

Guiding Those Left Behind In Ohio

2nd Edition

CONTENTS

About The Book

We tried to make this book as comprehensive as possible so there are specialized sections of the book that do not apply to the general population and may not be of interest to you. The following GUIDE POSTS appear throughout the book. You can read the section if the situation applies to you or skip the section if it doesn't. Skipping the section will not affect the continuity of the book.

GUIDE POSTS

The SPOUSE POST means that the information provided is specifically for the spouse of the decedent. If the decedent was single, you can skip the section.

The CALL-A-LAWYER POST alerts you to a situation that may require the assistance of an attorney. See the end of this chapter for information about how to find a lawyer.

The CAUTION POST alerts you to a potential problem. It is followed by a suggestion about how to avoid the problem.

The SPECIAL SITUATION POST means that the information given in that paragraph applies to a particular event or situation; for example when the decedent dies a violent death. If the situation does not apply, you can skip the section.

The Organization of the Book

Guiding Those Left Behind refers to the things that need to be done in order to settle an Estate in Ohio. The purpose of this book is to guide the reader through that process. It explains:

1. How to tend to the funeral and burial
2. What agencies need to be notified
3. How to locate the decedent's property
4. What bills need (and do not need) to be paid
5. How to determine who is entitled to inherit the decedent's property
6. How to transfer the decedent's property to the proper beneficiary

We devoted a chapter to each of these six steps; and for those who are in charge of settling an Estate, we placed a CHECK LIST at the end of Chapter 6 summarizing things that need to be done. Once you read Chapters 1 through 6 you will be able to identify those problems that can happen when someone dies. Using those Chapters as a base, you can set up your own Estate Plan so that your family is not burdened by similar problems. The rest of the book (Chapters 7, 8 and 9) suggests different methods you can use to accomplish this goal.

GLOSSARY

This book is designed for the average reader. Legal terminology has been kept to a minimum. There is a glossary at the end of the book in the event you come across a legal term that is not familiar to you.

FICTITIOUS NAMES AND EVENTS

The examples in this book are based loosely on actual events; however, all names are fictitious; and the events, as portrayed, are fictitious.

Reading the Law

Where applicable, we identified the state statute or federal statute that is the basis of the discussion. We did this as a reference, and also to encourage the general public to read the law as it is written. Prior to the Internet the only way you could look up the law was to physically take yourself to the local courthouse law library or the law section of a public library. Today, all of the state and federal statutes are literally at your finger tips. They are just a mouse click away on the Internet.

To look up the law all you need is the address of the Web site and the identifying number of the statute.

 FEDERAL STATUTES
http://www4.law.cornell.edu/uscode

OHIO STATUTES
http://www.legislature.state.oh.us

The Ohio legislature has revised their law into some 32 Chapters using odd numbers only, i.e., Chapter 1, Chapter 3, Chapter 5, etc. Once you have the number of the statute, it is simple to look it up. The first two numbers represent the chapter. The remaining numbers represent the section within that chapter. For example, (ORC 3107.01) refers to Chapter 31, Section 7.01 of the Ohio Revised Code.

If you come across a topic that is of importance to you, then you may find it both interesting and profitable to actually read the law as written.

Michael Joseph O'Brien, Esq.

MICHAEL JOSEPH O'BRIEN is a founding partner of Cleveland-based The O'Brien Law Firm LLC. The firm emphasizes estate and trust planning, probate, corporate planning, family business, family limited partnerships, charitable trusts, private family foundation planning and asset protection planning. He has a particular expertise in planning for families with children with disabilities.

Mr. O'Brien is a graduate Holy Cross College and the Cleveland-Marshall College of Law. He is admitted to practice in Ohio and Florida. He has administered many Florida estates with attention to special probate and tax concerns involving property disposition in multiple states. Mr. O'Brien is married with three children.

Mr. O'Brien is a member of the National Academy of Elder Law Attorneys, Inc. ("NAELA"), a non-profit association composed of attorneys who are experienced and trained in working with the legal problems of aging Americans and individuals of all ages with disabilities.

Michael Joseph O'Brien also belongs to the AMERICAN ACADEMY OF ESTATE PLANNING ATTORNEYS and regularly provides free educational seminars on the subject of Estate Planning.

About the Academy

The American Academy of Estate Planning Attorneys is a member organization serving the needs of legal professionals concentrating on Estate Planning. Through the Academy's comprehensive training and educational programs on state-of-the-art Estate Planning law and techniques, it fosters excellence in Estate Planning among its members and helps them deliver the highest possible service to their clients. The Academy provides its members with excellent legal education, and top notch practice management support. In addition, each member is required to attain thirty-six units of continuing legal education annually.

The American Academy of Estate Planning Attorneys serves law firms in forty-four states. Clients who choose an attorney who is a member of the Academy can feel confident that they have an attorney who is dedicated to bringing them the highest quality of service.

The Academy is also committed to educating consumers on vital Estate Planning issues that touch their lives. Through its series of publications, educational programs and its consumer Web site, the Academy seeks to create a public armed with the information they need to become wise consumers of Estate Planning services. You can learn more about Mr. O'Brien and the American Academy of Estate Planning Attorneys on the Internet.

THE ACADEMY: http://www.aaepa.com

Amelia E. Pohl, Esq.

Before becoming an attorney in 1985, AMELIA E. POHL taught mathematics on both the high school and college level. During her tenure as Associate Professor of Mathematics at Prince George's Community College in Maryland, she wrote several books including

Probability: A Set Theory Approach
Principals of Counting
Common Stock Sense

Ms. Pohl, graduated from Nova Law School in Florida and established an Elder Law practice. Over the years she observed that many people want to reduce the high cost of legal fees by performing or assisting with their own legal transactions. Attorney Pohl found that, with a bit of guidance, people are able to perform many legal transactions for themselves. Attorney Pohl utilizes her background as teacher, author and attorney to provide that "bit of guidance" to the general public in the form of self-help legal books that she has written. Amelia E. Pohl is currently completing this series for the remaining states:

Guiding Those Left Behind in Maine
Guiding Those Left Behind In Utah
Guiding Those Left Behind In Nevada, etc.

ACKNOWLEDGMENT

When someone dies, the family attorney is often among the first to be called. Family members have questions about whether probate is necessary, who to notify, how to get possession of the assets, etc. Over the years, as we practiced in the field of Elder Law, we noticed that the questions raised were much the same family to family. We both agreed that a book answering such questions would be of service to the general public.

We also observed, that those who had experience in settling the Estate of a loved one were more understanding of the process, and better able to make decisions about how to arrange their own finances to avoid problems that could arise in settling an Estate. We named the book *Guiding Those Left Behind*. The "Guiding" refers to the guidance that this book gives in the event you need to settle the Estate of a loved one. It also refers to the guidance that you can give to your family by setting up your own Estate Plan so your family is not burdened by unnecessary costs and delays in settling your Estate. We wish to thank all of the clients, who we have had the honor and pleasure to serve, for providing us with the impetus to produce this book.

THE DESIGN ARTIST

LUBOSH CECH designed the cover of this book. He is a renowned artist, with extensive educational background and professional work experience. Lubosh Cech is the founder of OKO DESIGN STUDIO located in Portland, Oregon. For more information about OKO Design Studio visit its Web site. http://www.okodesignstudio.com

The photograph on the cover was provided by the Nebraska Game and Parks Commission.

When You Need A Lawyer

The purpose of the book is to give the reader a basic understanding of what needs to be done when someone dies in Ohio, and to provide information about how a person can arrange his own affairs to avoid problems for his own family. It is not intended as a substitute for legal counsel or any other kind of professional advice. If you have any legal question, you should seek the counsel of an attorney. When looking for an attorney, consider three things: EXPERIENCE, COST and PERSONALITY.

EXPERIENCE

As of July, 2006, there are seven specialization programs offered by the Ohio State Bar Association::
   Estate Planning, Trust & Probate Law
   Family Relations Law
   Labor & Employment Law
   Real Property — Business, Commercial and Industrial Law
   Real Property — Residential Law
   Workers' Compensation Law

To become a *certified specialist* in these areas of law, the attorney must be experienced in the field, pass a written examination, and prove financial responsibility by having professional liability insurance.

Certification is just one of the criteria to consider. Many fine attorneys are knowledgable in an area of law, but the attorney have not taken the time, effort or expense to become certified as a specialist. If the attorney is not certified in the branch of law you seek, then ask how long he has practiced that type of law and what percentage of his practice is devoted to that branch of law.

You can call your local county Bar Association for a referral to an attorney. The Ohio State Bar Association has a Web site that gives the telephone numbers for each county Bar Association.

OHIO STATE BAR ASSOCIATION
http://www.ohiobar.org

One of the most reliable ways to find an attorney is through personal referral. Ask your friends, family or business acquaintances if they used an attorney for the field of law that you seek and whether they were pleased with the results. It is important to employ an attorney who is experienced in the area of law you seek. Your friend may have a wonderful Estate Planning attorney, but if you suffered an injury to your body, then you need an attorney who is experienced in Personal Injury.

COST

In addition to the attorney's experience, it is important to check what it will cost in attorney's fees. When you call for an appointment ask what the attorney will charge for the initial consultation and the approximate cost for the service you seek. Ask whether there will be additional costs such as filing fees, accounting fees, expert witness fees, etc.

If the least expensive attorney is out of your price range you can call the Ohio State Bar at (800) 282-6556 for the telephone number of the Legal Aid or Legal Services office nearest you.

The Ohio State Bar has a statewide Pro Seniors Legal Hotline and Referral Service for persons over 60. For information about the program call (800) 488-6070.

PERSONALITY

Of equal importance to the attorney's experience and legal fees, is your relationship with the attorney. How easy was it to reach the attorney? Did you go through layers of receptionists and legal assistants before being allowed to speak to the attorney? Did the attorney promptly return your call? If you had difficulty reaching the attorney, then you can expect similar problems should you employ that attorney.

Did the attorney treat you with respect? Did the attorney treat you paternally with a "father knows best" attitude or did he treat you as an intelligent person with the ability to understand the options available to you and the ability to make your own decision based on the information provided to you?

Are you able to understand and easily communicate with the attorney? Is he speaking to you in plain English or is his explanation of the matter so full of legalese to be almost meaningless to you?

Do you find the attorney's personality to be pleasant or grating? Sometimes people rub each other the wrong way. It is like rubbing a cat the wrong way. Stroking a cat from head to tail is pleasing to the cat, but petting it in the opposite direction, no matter how well intended, causes friction. If the lawyer makes you feel annoyed or uncomfortable, then find another attorney.

It is worth the effort to take the time to interview as many attorneys as it takes to find one with the right expertise, fee schedule and personality for you.

The First Week

Dealing with the death of a close family member or friend is difficult. Not only do you need to deal with your own emotions, but often with those of your family and friends. Sometimes their sorrow is more painful to you than what you are experiencing yourself.

In addition to the emotional impact of a death, there are many things that need to be done, from arranging the funeral and burial, to closing out the business affairs of the *decedent* (the person who died) and finally giving whatever property is left to the proper beneficiary.

The funeral and burial take only a few days. Wrapping up the affairs of the decedent may take considerably longer. This chapter explains what things you (the spouse or closest family member) need to do during the first week, beginning at the moment of death and continuing through the funeral.

 MALE GENDER USED

Rather than use "he/she" or "his/her" for simplicity
(and hoping not to offend anyone)
we will refer to the decedent and his
Personal Representative using the male gender.

References to other people will be in both genders.

AUTOPSIES

In today's high tech world of medicine, doctors are fairly certain of the cause of death, but if there is a question as to the cause of death, the doctor may ask for permission to perform an autopsy. Whoever has the right to dispose of the body may give consent (ORC 2108.50). Ohio statute gives a competent adult the right to sign a document appointing someone to be his **Representative For Disposition of Bodily Remains** (ORC 2108.72). If the decedent appointed a Representative, that person may give consent for the examination, provided the decedent did not direct the Representative to oppose an optional autopsy.

If no Representative was appointed, or if the Representative is unwilling or unable to take responsibility for the decedent's final disposition, then those with priority to give consent are as follows:

1st the surviving spouse 2nd all adult children
3rd the parents
4th all siblings, including those of the half blood
5th the grandparents
6th *descendants* (child, grandchild, great-grand child, etc.) of the deceased grandparents
7th anyone serving as the decedent's court appointed Guardian at time of his death
8th anyone willing to take responsibility for the disposition, including the person appointed by the Court to settle the decedent's Estate (ORC 2108.81).

The majority of persons in a given class shall decide whether to have the autopsy performed. If a majority cannot reach a decision, the Probate Court will decide the matter (ORC 2108.79).

The person who authorizes the autopsy must agree to pay for it because the cost of the examination is not covered under most health insurance plans. And that cost could be sizeable, running anywhere from several hundred to several thousand dollars, but it may be in the family's best interest to consent to the autopsy. The examination might reveal a genetic disorder that could be treated if it later appears in another family member. Death from a car "accident" could have been a heart attack at the wheel. Perhaps the patient who died suddenly in a hospital was misdiagnosed. The nursing home resident could have died from negligence and not old age. Even if none of these are found, knowing the cause of death with certainty is better than not knowing.

That was the case with the family of an elderly woman who was taken to the hospital complaining of stomach pains. The doctors thought she might be suffering from gallbladder disease but she died before they could effectively treat her. A doctor suggested that an autopsy be performed to determine the exact cause of death.
The woman had three daughters, one of whom objected to the autopsy: "Why spend that kind of money?
It won't bring Mom back."
The daughter's wishes were respected, however over the years as they aged and became ill with their own various ailments, they would undergo physical examinations. As part of taking their medical history, doctors routinely asked "And what was the cause of your mother's death?" None could answer the question.

This is not a dramatic story. No mysterious genetic dis-order ever occurred in any of her daughters, nor in any of their children. But each daughter (including the one who objected) at some point in her life, was confronted with the nagging question "What did Mom die of?"

AUTOPSIES PERFORMED BY CORONER

When a person dies, a physician, or his authorized agent, must sign the death certificate stating the cause of death. If a person dies in a hospital, a hospital official is there to sign the certificate. If a person dies at home from natural causes and he is under the care of a physician, the physician can sign the death certificate. In such case, there is no need to call 911. The funeral director will take possession of the body and obtain a *Burial Permit* from the local registrar of Vital Statistics (ORC 3705.17).

A law enforcement officer must be summoned whenever a body is discovered who was not under the care of a physician, or who died suddenly from illness, accident, suicide or foul play. The officer will ask the Coroner to determine the cause of death. If there is suspicion that the death was the result of a homicide or if the decedent died from a disease that poses an immediate and substantial threat to the public health, the Coroner will perform an autopsy or arrange to have one performed.

If a friend or family member objects to the autopsy on the grounds that such examination is against the religious beliefs of the decedent, the Coroner will give that person 48 hours within which to file a petition with the Court of Common Pleas to prevent the procedure. However, if it is suspected that the death was the result of murder, the Coroner has the right to immediately proceed with the autopsy, regardless of the religious belief of the decedent (ORC 313.131).

If the Coroner is not investigating a homicide, but he believes there is a compelling public necessity to conduct the autopsy, he can file his own motion asking the Court to waive the 48 hour period and allow him to proceed with the examination. Upon the filing of the Coroner's petition, the Court will contact the family, hear their objections, and then rule on the matter (ORC 313.131).

The cost of an autopsy performed by the state is paid for by the county in which the body was found (ORC 313.161). Once the Coroner takes possession of a body, it will not be released until the examination is complete. In the interim, the family can proceed with arrangements for the funeral. The funeral director will contact the Coroner to determine when he can pick up the body and proceed with funeral arrangements.

AUTOPSIES PERFORMED BY THE INSURANCE COMPANY
A company that issues accident and sickness insurance in the state of Ohio is required to include a provision in their policy stating that the company has the right to perform an autopsy (ORC 3923.04 (J)). The cost of the autopsy is paid for by the insurance company, so they will not order an autopsy unless there is some important reason to do so.

ANATOMICAL GIFTS

Hospital personnel determine whether a mortally ill patient is a candidate for an organ donation. Early on in the donor program those over 65 were not considered as suitable candidates. Today, however, the condition of the organ, and not the age, is the determining factor.

The federal government has established regional Organ Procurement Organizations throughout the United States to coordinate the donor program: LifeBanc services Northeastern Ohio; Life Connection of Ohio services Northwestern and West Central Ohio; Lifeline of Ohio Organ Procurement Agency services Central and Southeastern Ohio; LifeCenter services Southwestern Ohio. The Kentucky Organ Donor Affiliates services Lawrence County, Ohio. If it is decided that the patient is a candidate, the hospital will contact the local Organ Procurement Organization.

GIFT AUTHORIZED PRIOR TO DEATH
If, before death, the decedent made an anatomical gift by signing an Organ Donor Card, the hospital personnel or the donor's doctor need to be made aware of the gift in quick proximity to the time of death — preferably before death. If it is determined that the donation is medically acceptable, the gift will be made. No family member needs to give permission, provided the hospital has a copy of the decedent's unrevoked Donor Card.

GIFT AUTHORIZED BY THE FAMILY
If no Organ Donor Card is on record, and it is determined that the decedent is a suitable donor, someone who is specially trained will approach the family to request permission for the donation.

Ohio statute states an order of priority for those who can give permission:

1st   the surviving spouse   2nd   adult son or daughter
3rd   either parent   4th   adult brother or sister
5th   a grandparent
6th   the decedent's court appointed Guardian (if any)
7th   Anyone else authorized to dispose of the body

Every effort must be made to contact those people with highest priority. No gift can be made if someone agrees to the gift and someone with higher priority objects. For example, if the sister of the decedent agrees to the gift (4th in priority) and the decedent had an adult child (2nd in priority), then the child needs to be made aware of the gift. No gift can be made if the child objects. Similarly, the statute prohibits the gift if the decedent, prior to death, refused to make a gift, or ever expressed an objection to someone with authority to make the gift (ORC 2108.02).

AFTER THE DONATION

Once the donation is made, the body is delivered to the funeral home and prepared for burial or cremation as directed by the family. The donation does not disfigure the body so there can be an open casket viewing if the family so wishes.

Some regional Organ Procurement Organizations have an aftercare program that includes a letter of condolence to the family and an expression of gratitude for the gift. For privacy reasons, the identity of the recipient of the gift is not disclosed, but on request from the family, the local Organ Procurement Organization will give the family basic demographic information about the donation, such as the age, sex, marital status, number of children and occupation of the recipient of the gift.

Consider offering to release the body for the purpose of education or research in the event that the decedent signed a donor card, but was not an appropriate candidate for an organ donation. There are donation programs in several schools throughout the state. You need to call the school within 24 hours of the death to determine whether they will accept the body. They will not accept bodies from those who weigh more than 300 pounds or have died from a contagious disease or from crushing injuries.

Each school has their own polices and procedures:
The Anatomy Department of Ohio State University
at Columbus, Ohio   (614) 292-4831
does not pay to transport the body to the school, so you need to pay to have a funeral director transport the body to the school.

The College of Osteopathic Medicine of the Ohio University
at Athens, Ohio   (740) 593-2171
will pay for the transportation of the body, provided it is within 150 miles of the school.

The Department of Anatomy at Case Western
Reserve University at Cleveland, Ohio   (216) 368-3430
requires advance registration by the decedent. They will not accept a donation even if the next of kin or Health Care Agent authorize the study.

The study can take up to two years to complete. At the end of the study the remains are cremated. The *cremains* (cremated remains) will be placed in a cemetery local to the university; or if the family wishes, the cremains will be delivered to them. Some schools will mail the cremains without charge. The Anatomy Department of Ohio State at Columbus charges $125 to send the cremains.

CAVEAT: Federal law prohibits payment for organ donations (42 U.S.C. 274 e). There is no ban on payments made to prepare organs or tissue for transplantation, nor is there any ban on charges made to transport bodies or body parts. Not-for-profit, as well as for-profit, companies have sprung up that are in the business of preparing and delivering body parts. These companies request donations from families — so they are not violating federal law by paying for the donation. The company prepares the body tissue or other parts of the donated body, and then distributes the parts throughout the United States to physicians, hospitals, research centers, etc. In many cases the monies charged for preparation and transportation includes a sizable profit.

If a company or organization, other than your local Organ Procurement Organization, approaches you to make a donation, before agreeing you may want to learn about the company making the request.

What is the name of the company?
Where are their main headquarters located?
What is their primary business activity?
What is the name and job description of the
person making the request?

DETERMINE THE END USE OF THE DONATION

You may want to ask what they intend to do with the tissue or body part. If it is being used for research, what type of research? Where is the research being conducted? If it will be used for transplantation, what agency (doctor, hospital) will receive the donation and where is that agency located?

Once you have this information you can make an informed decision as to whether you wish to make the donation to that organization.

THE FUNERAL

Approximately ten percent of deaths occur suddenly because of accident, suicide, foul play or undetected illness. But, in general, death occurs after a lengthy illness, with a common scenario being that of an aged person who dies after being ill for several months, if not years. In such case, family and friends are prepared for the happening. Expected or not, the first job is the disposition of the body.

THE PREARRANGED FUNERAL

Increasingly, people are arranging, in advance, for their own funeral and burial. This makes it easier on the family both financially and emotionally. All the decisions have been made and there is no guessing what the decedent would have wanted.

If the decedent made provision for his burial, you should come across a cemetery deed or perhaps a certificate for a burial plot. If he made provision for his funeral, you should find a PRENEED FUNERAL CONTRACT. You need to read the contract to determine what arrangements were made. If the contract was being paid by installment, determine whether it is paid in full.

If you cannot find a Preneed Funeral Contract, but you know the decedent made provision for his burial and funeral, call the funeral home and ask them to send you a copy of the contract. If you believe the decedent purchased a funeral plan but you do not know the name of the funeral home, call the local funeral homes. Many local funeral homes are owned by national firms with computer capacity to identify people who have purchased a Preneed Funeral plan at any of their many locations.

Once you have a copy of the contract, take it with you to the funeral home and go over the terms of the agreement with the funeral director. Determine whether the contract was a fixed price agreement or whether there will be additional charges.

MAKING FUNERAL ARRANGEMENTS

If the decedent died unexpectedly or without having made any prior funeral arrangements, your first job is to choose a funeral director and make arrangements for the funeral or cremation. Many people choose the nearest or most conveniently located funeral home without comparison shopping. However, prices for these services can vary significantly from funeral home to funeral home. Savings can be had if you take the time to make a few phone calls.

Receiving price quotes by telephone is your right under Federal law. Federal Trade Commission ("FTC") Rule 453.2 (b) (1) requires a funeral director to give an accurate telephone quote of the prices of his goods and services. Funeral homes are listed in the telephone directory under FUNERAL DIRECTORS. If you live in a small town, there may be only one or two listings. If such is the case, check out some funeral homes in the next largest city.

Funeral directors usually provide the following services:
➢ arrange for the transportation of the body to the funeral home and then to the burial site
➢ obtain a burial transit permit
➢ arrange for the embalming or cremation of the body
➢ arrange funeral and memorial services and the viewing of the body
➢ obtain information for the death certificate
➢ order copies of the death certificate for the family
➢ have memorial cards printed.

To compare prices you will need to determine:
- ✧ what is included in the price of a basic funeral plan
- ✧ whether you can expect any additional cost.

It may be necessary to have the body embalmed if you are going to have a viewing. Embalming is not necessary if you order a direct cremation or an immediate burial without a viewing. Federal Trade Commission Rule 453.5 prohibits the funeral home from charging an embalming fee unless you order the service.

If the decedent did not own a burial space, then that cost must be included when making funeral arrangements.

PURCHASING THE CASKET

When comparison-shopping, you will find that the single most expensive item in the funeral arrangement is the casket. Most funeral directors will quote you a price for a basic funeral plan that does not include the cost of the casket. Directors usually quote a range of prices for the casket, saying that you will need to come in and choose the casket at the time you contract for the funeral.

When selecting a casket you need to be aware that there may be a considerable mark-up in the price quoted by the funeral director. You do not need to go "sole source" when purchasing the casket. You can purchase the casket elsewhere and have it delivered to the funeral home to be used instead of the one offered by the funeral director. Funeral homes are required to accept caskets purchased elsewhere, and they may not charge a handling fee for accepting that casket. But if the price list given to you by the funeral home states that the price of their casket includes a specific dollar amount for basic services, then the funeral director is allowed to add that dollar amount to the charge for his services, should you purchase the casket elsewhere (FTC Rule 453.2, 453.4).

Caskets are not usually displayed for sale in a shopping mall, so most of us have no idea of the going price for a casket. With the advent of the Internet, you can learn all about the cost of any item, even a casket, by using your search engine to find a retail casket sales dealer. If you are not computer literate, you can locate the nearest retail casket sales outlet by looking in the yellow pages under CASKETS. You may need to look in the telephone directory for the nearest large city to find a listing. By making a call to a retail casket sales dealer, you will become knowledgeable in the price range of caskets. You can then decide what is a reasonable price for the product you seek.

The best time to do your comparison shopping is before you go to the funeral home to arrange for the funeral. Once you have determined what you should pay for the casket, it is only fair to give the funeral director the opportunity to meet that price. If you cannot reach a meeting of the minds, then you can always order the casket from the retail sales dealer and have it delivered to the funeral home.

ON-LINE FUNERAL SERVICES

The Internet is changing the way the world does business, and the funeral industry is no exception. A growing number of mortuaries are offering live Webcasts of funerals and wakes for those who are unable to pay their respects in person.

There are Web sites where you can post an obituary. There are on-line memorial chat rooms as well as on-line eulogies and testimonials. There is even a Website that offers a posthumous e-mail service which allows people to leave final messages for friends and relatives. You can locate these services using your favorite search engine and typing in "obituaries."

THE CREMATION

Increasingly people are opting for cremation. The reasons for choosing cremation are varied, but for many, it is a matter of finances. The cost of cremation is approximately one-sixth that of an ordinary funeral and burial. A major saving is the cost of the casket. A casket is not necessary for the cremation and Federal law prohibits a Funeral Director from saying that a casket is required for a direct cremation (FTC Rule 453.3 (b)ii). You may need a suitable container to deliver the body to the crematory. After the cremation, you will need an urn for the ashes.

If you are having a memorial service in a place of worship and no viewing of the body before the cremation, then consider contracting with a facility that does cremations only. Look in the telephone book under CREMATION SERVICES. You will also see cremation "societies" in the telephone book. Some are for-profit and others not-for-profit. You can also find advertisements for cremation services on the Internet.

PRELIMINARY CONSIDERATIONS

Under Ohio law, certain things are required before the cremation may take place:

24 HOURS FROM TIME OF DEATH
No cremation may take place until at least 24 hours from the date of death (as listed on the death certificate) has passed (ORC 4717.23 (A)(1)).

BURIAL OR BURIAL-TRANSIT PERMIT
The funeral or cremation director must obtain a Burial Permit, or a Burial-Transit Permit prior to performing the cremation (ORC 3705.17, 4717.23(A)(2)).

THE OVERWEIGHT DECEDENT

Cremation technology has kept up with the expanding waist line of our population. Most Cremation Services can accommodate a body weighing up to 400 pounds. But if the decedent is extremely obese, you need to check to see whether the Cremation service has facilities large enough to handle the body. If you cannot locate a crematory that can accommodate the body, you will need to make burial arrangements.

THE DECEDENT WITH A PACEMAKER

Cremating a body with a pacemaker or any radiation producing device can cause damage to the cremation chamber or to the person performing the cremation. If the decedent was wearing such electronic aid, you need to make arrangements with the cemetery director for its removal.

Some veterinary hospitals are implanting used pace makers into pets who are suffering from heart disease. If the decedent was an animal advocate, consider making a donation of the pacemaker, in his memory, to the hospital.

WRITTEN AUTHORIZATION

Ohio law requires written authorization for the cremation. The contents of the *Authorization Form* must contain all of the information as required in Ohio statute (ORC 4717.24). The statute is four pages long and contains information about the decedent and his final disposition. Whoever signs the Authorization Form must verify that the decedent's body does not contain any mechanical or radioactive devise or implant that might pose a hazard to those performing the cremation.

Whoever has the right to provide for the decedent's final disposition may sign the Authorization form (see page 2) (ORC 4717.22).

DISPOSING OF THE CREMAINS

The authorization form for the cremation contains a section that gives instructions for the final disposition of the cremains. If you do not fill in that section, the operator of the crematory is required to return the cremains to you after 30 days. If he cannot locate you, then any time after 60 days, he can place the cremains in a grave, crypt or niche and bill the cost of the final disposition to you (ORC 4717.27).

If the cremains are to be placed in a cemetery, you need to obtain a suitable urn for the burial. The container provided by the crematory can be used, or you can purchase an urn from the funeral director or crematory service director. Urns cost much less than caskets, but they can cost several hundred dollars. You may wish to do some comparison shopping by calling a retail sales casket dealer.

Many cemeteries have a separate section or building called a *columbarium*, which is especially designed to store urns. Some cemeteries allow the cremains of a family member to be placed in an occupied family plot or mausoleum If you wish to have the cremains placed in an occupied mausoleum or family plot, you need to call the cemetery and ask them to explain their policy as it relates to the burial of urns in an occupied site.

SCATTERED AT SEA

The decedent may have expressed a desire to have his ashes placed at sea. The funeral director or cremation director should be able to assist you in seeing to it that these wishes are respected. Federal law prohibits the ashes from being scattered any closer than three nautical miles from land, so you will need to arrange to have a boat carry the ashes out to sea (Code of Federal Regulations, Title 40, Section 229.1).

If the decedent is to be buried in another state, you will need to arrange for the transportation of the body to that state. Many states, including Ohio, require a Burial-Transit Permit for burial or removal from the state where the death occurred. The funeral director in Ohio, will obtain a Burial-Transit Permit from the local Registrar (ORC 3705.17).

If services are to be held in Ohio and in another state, contact a local funeral director and he will make arrangements with the out-of-state funeral home for the transportation of the body. If you do not plan to have services conducted in Ohio, you can contact the out-of-state funeral director and ask him to effect the transfer. Many funeral home belong to a national network of funeral homes, so both the local and the out-of-state funeral director usually have the means to make arrangements to transport the body.

TRANSPORTING CREMAINS

If the body has been cremated, you can transport the cremains yourself, either by carrying the ashes as part of your luggage or by arranging with the airline to transport the ashes as cargo. Have a certified copy of the death certificate and the Burial-Transit Permit ready in the event that you need to identify the cremains of the decedent.

In these days of heightened security, it is important to call the airline before departure and ask whether they have any special regulation or procedure regarding the transportation of human ashes.

SPOUSE ▶ THE MILITARY BURIAL

Subject to availability of burial spaces, an honorably discharged veteran and his dependent child and his unremarried spouse may be buried in a national military cemetery. Some cemeteries are closed to new internments, however, they may have room for cremated remains or for the casketed remains of a family member of someone currently buried in that cemetery.

The two national military cemeteries located in Ohio have space available for new internments.

Dayton National Cemetery
VA Medical Center
4100 West Third Street
Dayton, OH 45428-1008
Telephone: (937) 262-2115

Ohio Western Reserve National Cemetery
10175 Rawiga Road
P.O. Box 8
Rittman, OH 44270
Telephone (330) 335-3069

ARLINGTON NATIONAL CEMETERY
An honorably discharged veteran can be buried in the national military cemetery at Arlington, Virginia. The Department of the Army is in charge of the Arlington National Cemetery. You can call the **Interment Service Branch** at (703) 607-8585 for information about having a Veteran buried there.

THE COST OF A
MILITARY BURIAL

Burial space in a National Cemetery is free of charge. Cemetery employees will open and close the grave and mark it with a headstone or grave marker without cost to the family. If requested, the local Veteran's Administration ("VA") will provide the family with a memorial flag. The VA will not pay to have the body transported to the cemetery, so the family needs to make arrangements with a funeral firm to transport the remains to the cemetery.

Regardless of where an honorably discharged veteran is buried, allowances may be available for the plot, and the burial and grave marker expenses. The amount varies depending on factors such as whether the veteran died because of a service related injury. The VA will not reimburse any burial or funeral expense for the spouse of a veteran. For information about reimbursement of funeral and burial expenses you can call the VA at (800) 827-1000.

The Department of Veteran's Affairs has a Website with information on the following topics:
- ➤ National and Military Cemeteries
- ➤ Burial, Headstones and Markers
- ➤ State Cemetery Grants Program
- ➤ Obtaining Military Records
- ➤ Locating Veterans

 VA CEMETERY WEB SITE
http://www.cem.va.gov

| SPOUSE | | BENEFITS FOR SPOUSE
OF DECEASED VETERAN |

The surviving spouse of an honorably discharged veteran should contact the Veteran's Administration to determine whether he/she is eligible for any benefits. For example, if the decedent had minor or disabled children, his spouse may also be eligible for a monthly benefit of Dependency and Indemnity Compensation ("DIC").

Whether a surviving spouse is eligible for benefits depends on many factors including whether the decedent was serving on active duty, whether his death was service related, and the surviving spouse's assets and income. DIC benefits are discontinued should the surviving spouse remarry; however, the law allows payments to be resumed in the event that the subsequent marriage ends because of death or divorce.

For information about whether the surviving spouse is eligible for any benefit related to the decedent's military service call the VA at (800) 827-1000.

You can receive a printed statement of public policy: VA Pamphlet 051-000-00228-8 FEDERAL BENEFITS FOR VETERANS AND DEPENDENTS by sending a $7 check to:
THE SUPERINTENDENT OF DOCUMENTS
P.O. Box 371954
Pittsburgh, PA 15250-7954
Or you can download it without charge from the Internet.

 VETERAN'S ADMINISTRATION
http://www.va.gov

 **LAWYER**   THE WRONGFUL DEATH

It is important to have a Personal Injury attorney or Products Liability attorney investigate any accidental death, to determine whether the death was caused by the wrongful act of a person, or company. If the accident was related to the decedent's job, the family may wish to consult with a Worker's Compensation attorney as well.

The person appointed by the Court to settle the decedent's Estate will sue on behalf of the decedent's surviving spouse, children and parents; and if none of these, the decedent's next of kin. The next of kin are determined according to Ohio's Laws of Descent and Distribution.

Family members have the right to be compensated for any economic loss, including lost financial support, they suffer because of a *wrongful death* (a death caused by a wrongful act). They are also entitled to compensation for loss of companionship, loss of the decedent's services, and mental anguish suffered because of the loss. The Court or the jury, in the case of a jury trial, will decide the amount each family member will receive.

The Court or the jury may award reasonable funeral and burial expenses incurred as a result of the wrongful death (ORC 2125.02).

VICTIMS OF CRIME COMPENSATION PROGRAM

The State of Ohio reimburses crime victims and/or their dependents, or immediate family members, who suffer loses that are not covered by insurance, public funds or any other compensation (ORC 2743.51). If the decedent died because of a crime, including an accident caused by drunk driving, you may be eligible to be reimbursed for loses under the **OHIO VICTIMS OF CRIME COMPENSATION PROGRAM**. Compensation can be awarded for funeral and burial expenses (up to $2,500), for medical expenses, psychological counseling, lost support, lost wages, etc. Total compensation may not exceed $50,000 (ORC 2743.60).

The Office of the Ohio Attorney General administers the program (ORC 2743.59). In general, to be eligible, the following must be true:

➢ The decedent was an innocent victim.

➢ The *claimant* (applicant) was an innocent victim.

➢ The crime was reported to authorities within 72 hours of the discovery of the body.

➢ The application for compensation was filed within two years from the commission of the crime or discovery of the body (ORC 2743.56).

You can pick up an application for compensation at any law enforcement agency or you can call (800) 582-2877 and they will mail it to you, or you can download the application from the Internet.

THE OHIO ATTORNEY GENERAL
http://www.ag.state.oh.us/victim

THE UNCLAIMED BODY

Police make every effort to identify and locate the family of an unclaimed body. If an indigent person dies and the police know his identity, they will try to locate the family. If the identity of the decedent is unknown, or if his family is unable or unwilling to arrange for his burial, the officer of the township or municipal corporation where the body was found will have the body buried or cremated at the expense of the township or municipal corporation (ORC 5101.521).

If the decedent died while at a facility supported in whole or part at public expense (county home, correctional facility, city hospital, etc.), and the body is unidentified, or not accepted by the family within 36 hours of the death, the person in possession of the body (superintendent, sheriff, coroner, director, etc.) will offer the body to a school of medicine for the purpose of study and research (ORC 1713.34).

THE INDIGENT VETERAN
As explained previously, an honorably discharged veteran can be buried without charge — with the exception of transportation costs to the veteran's cemetery.

Special Situation >	THE PROBLEM FUNERAL OR BURIAL

The funeral and burial industry is well regulated by both state and federal government. Under Ohio statue (ORC 4717.04) the following acts are subject to disciplinary action:

⊠ Misleading the public by using false or deceptive advertising, such as delivering goods of a lesser quality than that presented to the purchaser as a sample

⊠ Committing unprofessional conduct

⊠ Refusing to release a body to someone who is legally entitled to it

Funeral directors are licensed professionals so it is unusual to have a problem with the funeral or burial or cremation. If, however, you had a bad experience with any aspect of the funeral then you can file a complaint with the state licensing agency:

Board of Embalmers and Funeral Directors of Ohio
77 S High Street, 16th Floor
Columbus, OH 43226-0313
(614) 466-4252

In addition to filing a complaint with the Board, you may wish to consult with an attorney who is experienced in litigation matters to learn of any other legal remedy that you may have.

Few things are more difficult to deal with than a missing person. The emotional turmoil created by the "not knowing" is often more difficult than the finality of death. The legal problems created by the disappearance are also more difficult than if the person simply died. It may take a three-part legal process — the appointment of someone to manage the missing person's finances, a hearing to determine whether to presume that he is dead, and finally, the Probate procedure.

APPOINTING A TRUSTEE

An *Absentee* is a person who is missing and cannot be found after a diligent search. If the Absentee has been missing for at least three months, and business matters need attending (bills that need to be paid, family to be supported, etc.), his spouse or next of kin can ask the Probate Court to appoint a *Trustee* of the Absentee's property. The Trustee will manage the property, under Court supervision, until the Absentee can be found (ORC 2119.01).

BEGINNING PROBATE

Any time there is sufficient to evidence that the Absentee is dead, or if the federal government makes a finding of death under the Federal Missing Persons Act (37 U.S.C.A. 551), or once five years has passed, whoever has the right to inherit the Absentee's property can ask the Court to issue a decree of a presumption of death (ORC 2105.35, 2121.01). The judge will hear evidence to determine whether the missing person should be presumed dead, and if so, the Probate procedure can begin (ORC 2121.05).

THE DEATH CERTIFICATE

Whoever is in charge of the final disposition (usually the funeral director) will collect information about the decedent and report it to the local Registrar of Vital Statistics in the district where the death occurred (ORC 3705.16). The Registrar will prepare a death record based on that information and report it to the Ohio Department of Health, Office of Vital Statistics (ORC 3705.02, 3705.07). It is important that the information you give to the funeral director is correct. You need to check the form completed by the funeral director to be sure names are correctly spelled and dates correctly written. Once the information is sent to the Department of Health, it will be difficult and time consuming to make a correction.

The funeral director will order as many certified copies of the death record as you request. Most establishments require an original certified copy and not a photocopy so you need to order sufficient certified copies. The following is a list of institutions that may request a certified copy:

* Each insurance company that insured the decedent or his property (health insurance, life insurance, car insurance, etc.)
* Each financial institution in which the decedent had money invested (brokerage houses, banks)
* The decedent's pension fund
* Each credit card company used by the decedent
* The IRS
* The Social Security Administration
* The Bureau of Motor Vehicles
* If Probate is necessary, the Clerk of the Probate Court.

ORDERING COPIES OF THE DEATH CERTIFICATE

Some airlines and car rental companies offer a discount for short notice, emergency trips. If you have family flying in for the funeral, you may wish to order a few extra copies of the death certificate so that they can obtain an airline or car rental discount.

To order certified copies of the death certificate at a later date, you can call the funeral director and ask him to do so, or you can order a death certificate from the OHIO DEPARTMENT OF HEALTH Web site.

 OHIO DEPARTMENT OF HEALTH
http://www.odh.ohio.gov/vitalstatistics

LOCAL VITAL STATISTICS OFFICE
You can also obtain a certified copy of the death certificate from your County Health Department Office where the death occurred. You will find the address and telephone number of the County Office at the above Department of Health Web site.

BY MAIL
You can obtain a certified copy of the Death Record by writing to: Ohio Department of Health
Vital Statistics
246 N. High Street, 1st Floor, Revenue Room
P.O. Box 15098
Columbus, Ohio 43215-0098

It is a good idea to first call them at (614) 466-2531 to check the cost and ask what information they require.

WALK-IN
Same day service is available to walk-in customers.
Ohio Department of Health
Vital Statistics
225 Neilston Street
Columbus, Ohio 43215

You may want to first call for directions, office hours and cost of obtaining a copy of the death certificate.

About Probate

Once a person dies, all of the property he owns as of the date of his death is referred to as the **decedent's Estate.** If the decedent owned property that was in his name only (not jointly or in trust for someone), some sort of court procedure may be necessary to determine who is entitled to ownership of the property. The name of the court procedure is **Probate**.

In Ohio, Probate is conducted in the Probate Division of the *Court of Common Pleas* (ORC 2101.01). We will use the term Court" or "Probate Court" to refer to the judge who is presiding over Probate matters.

The root of the word Probate is "to prove." It refers to the first job of the Probate Court, that is, to examine proof of whether the decedent left a valid Will. The second job of the Probate Court is to appoint someone to wrap up the affairs of the decedent by paying the cost of the Probate procedure, any outstanding bills, and then distributing whatever is left to the proper beneficiary. If the decedent left a valid Will naming someone as *Executor* of his Estate, the Court will appoint that person for the job and issue *Letters Testamentary* giving him authority to administer the Estate.

If the decedent died without a Will, the Probate Court will appoint someone to be the *Administrator* of his Estate and issue *Letters of Administration.*

For simplicity, we will refer to the person appointed by the court to settle the decedent's Estate as the **Personal Representative**, and the document authorizing him to act, as **Letters** (ORC 2113.01).

There are different ways to conduct a Probate procedure depending on the value of the property that is being Probated, and whether the decedent owned real property at the time of his death. We will refer to the property that is distributed as part of a Probate proceeding as the decedent's **Probate Estate** and the method of conducting the Probate as the **Estate Administration**.

Chapter 6 explains the different kinds of Estate Administration that are available in the state of Ohio.

But we are getting ahead of ourselves. First we need to determine whether a Probate procedure is necessary. To answer that question we need to know exactly what the decedent owned, so the next two chapters explain how to identify, and then locate, the decedent's assets.

Giving Notice Of The Death 2

Those closest to the decedent usually notify family members and close friends by telephone. The funeral director will arrange to have an obituary published in as many different newspapers as the family requests, but there is still the job of notifying the government and people who were doing business with the decedent. That job is the duty of whoever is appointed as Personal Representative of the decedent's Estate.

Ohio law gives an order of priority for the appointment of Personal Representative. Whoever the decedent named as Executor or Personal Representative in his Will has top priority. Once appointed, it is his job to give notice of the death. If the decedent died without a valid Will, the surviving spouse has priority to be appointed as Personal Representative — provided the spouse is a resident of Ohio. If not, the job falls to his next of kin as determined by the Laws of Descent and Distribution who are residents of Ohio (ORC 2113.06).

Whoever takes the job of settling the decedent's Estate needs to give notice as soon as is practicable after the death. Two government agencies that need to be notified are the Social Security Administration and the IRS. This chapter gives their telephone numbers as well as other agencies that need to be notified.

NOTIFYING SOCIAL SECURITY

Many funeral directors will, as part of their service package, notify the Social Security Administration of the death. You may wish to check to see that this has been done. You can do so by calling (800) 772-1213. If you are hearing impaired call (800) 325-0778 TTY. You will need to give the Social Security Administration the full legal name of the decedent as well as his Social Security number and date of birth.

Special Situation | DECEDENT RECEIVING SOCIAL SECURITY

If the decedent was receiving checks from Social Security, you need to determine whether his last check needs to be returned to the Social Security Administration. Each Social Security check is a payment for the prior month, provided that person lives for the entire prior month. If the decedent died on the last day of the month, you should not cash the check for that month.

For example, if he died on July 31st, you need to return the check that the Social Security mailed out in August. If however, he died on August 1st the check sent in August need not be returned because that check was payment for the month of July.

If the Social Security check is electronically deposited into a bank account, notify the bank and the Social Security Administration that the account holder died. If the check needs to be returned, the Social Security Administration will withdraw it electronically from the bank account. You will need to keep the account open until the funds are withdrawn.

‖ SPOUSE ‖ ▸ SPOUSE/CHILD'S SOCIAL SECURITY BENEFITS

If the decedent had sufficient work credits, the Social Security Administration will give the decedent's widow(er) or if unmarried, then the decedent's minor children, a one-time death benefit in the amount of $255.

SURVIVORS BENEFITS:
The spouse (or former spouse) of the decedent may be eligible for Survivors Benefits. Benefits vary depending on the amount of work credits earned by the decedent; whether the decedent had minor or disabled children; the spouse's age; how long they were married; etc. The minor child of the decedent may be eligible for benefits regardless of whether the child's father (the decedent) ever married the child's mother. Paternity can be established by any one of several methods including the father acknowledging his child in writing or verbally to members of his family. For more information you can call the Social Security Administration at (800) 772-1213.

SOCIAL SECURITY BENEFITS
A spouse or former spouse can collect Social Security benefits based on the decedent's work record. This value may be greater than the spouse now receives. It is important to make an appointment with your local Social Security office and determine whether you as the spouse (or former spouse) or parent of decedent's minor child are eligible for any Social Security or Survivor benefit. You can down load publications that explain survivors benefits from the Social Security Web site.

 SOCIAL SECURITY ADMINISTRATION
http://www.socialsecurity.gov

| Special
Situation | DECEDENT WITH
GOVERNMENT PENSION |

DECEDENT WITH GOVERNMENT PENSION

Any pension or annuity check received after the date of death of a federal retiree, or a survivor annuitant, needs to be returned to the U.S. Treasury. If the check is direct deposited to a bank account, call the financial institution and ask them to return the check. If the check is sent by mail, you need to return it to the return mail address on the Department of Treasury envelope in which the check was mailed. Include a letter explaining the reason for the return of the check and stating the decedent's date of death.

$$$ APPLY FOR BENEFITS $$$

A survivor annuity may be available to a surviving spouse, and/or minor or disabled child. In some cases, a former spouse may be eligible for benefits. Even though you notify the government of the death, they will not automatically give you benefits to which you may be entitled. You need to apply for those benefits by notifying the Office of Personnel Management ("OPM") of the death and requesting that they send you an application for survivor benefits. You can call them at (888) 767-6738 or you can write to:

U. S. OFFICE OF PERSONNEL MANAGEMENT
RETIREMENT OPERATIONS CENTER
Post Office Box 45
Boyers, PA 16017-4500

You will find brochures and information about Survivor's Benefits at the OPM Website.

 U.S. OFFICE OF PERSONNEL MANAGEMENT
http://www.opm.gov

| Special Situation | DECEDENT WITH COMPANY PENSION OR ANNUITY |

In most cases, pension and annuity checks are payment for the prior month. If the decedent received his pension or annuity check before his death, then no monies need be returned. Pension checks and/or annuity checks received after the date of death may need to be returned to the company. You need to notify the company of the death to determine the status of the last check sent to the decedent.

Before notifying the company, locate the policy or pension statement that is the basis of the income. That document should tell whether there is a beneficiary of the pension or annuity funds now that the pensioner or annuitant is dead. If you cannot locate the document, use the return address on the check envelope and ask the company to send you a copy of the plan. Also request that they forward to you any claim form that may be required in order for the survivor or beneficiary to receive benefits under that pension plan or policy.

If the pension/annuity check is direct deposited to the decedent's account, then ask the bank to assist you in locating the company and notifying the company of the death.

Anyone who is a beneficiary of an Individual Retirement Account ("IRA") or QRP needs to keep in mind that income taxes may not have been paid on monies placed in an IRA or QRP account. In such case, significant taxes may be due when the money is withdrawn. You need to learn what options are available to you as a beneficiary of the plan and the tax consequences of each option. You will need to ask an accountant how much will be due in taxes for each option. Once you know all the facts, you will be able to make the best choice for your circumstance.

SPOUSE There are special options available if the spouse is the beneficiary of the decedent's IRA account. The spouse has the right to withdraw the money from the account or roll it over into the spouse's own retirement account. Although the employer can explain options that are available, the spouse still needs to understand the tax consequence of choosing any given option. It is important to consult with an accountant to determine the best way to go.

If the decedent had a QRP, the plan may permit the spouse to roll the balance of the account into a new IRA. The spouse needs to contact the decedent's employer for an explanation of the plan and all the options that are available at this time.

NOTIFYING IRS

THE FINAL INCOME TAX RETURN

The surviving spouse can file a final joint federal income tax return. If there is no surviving spouse, the Personal Representative will file the decedent's final return. If Probate is not necessary, whoever takes possession of the decedent's property needs to file the final return. The return needs to be filed by April 15th of the year following the death.

If the decedent earned an income, or even won the state lottery during the year of his death, an state income tax return must also be filed with the Ohio Tax Commissioner at the same time the federal return is filed 5747.08(G)). No return is due if the total credits allowed by Ohio statute is less than or equal to the amount of taxes due. The Ohio Income Tax Law is complex, especially as it relates to tax credits, so you may want to employ an accountant to assist with preparing the decedent's final return. You can also get information about filing the final Ohio return by calling the **OHIO DEPARTMENT OF TAXATION** at (800) 282-1780, or you can visit their Web site.

 OHIO DEPARTMENT OF TAXATION
http://www.tax.ohio.gov

You may want to keep the decedent's bank account open until you determine whether the decedent is entitled to an income tax refund. See Chapter 6 for an explanation of how to obtain a tax refund.

THE GOOD NEWS

Monies inherited from the decedent are generally not counted as income to you, so you do not pay federal income tax on those monies. If the monies you inherit later earn interest or income for you, then of course you will report that income as you do any other type of income.

Both the federal and state government have the right to impose an **Estate Tax** on property transferred to a beneficiary as a result of the death. All the property owned as of the date of death becomes the decedent's **Taxable Estate.** This includes *real property* (residential lots, condominiums etc.) and *personal property* (life insurance policies, cars, business interests, securities, IRA accounts, etc.). It includes property held in the decedent's name alone, as well as property that he held jointly or in Trust. It also includes gifts given by the decedent during his lifetime that exceeded **Annual Gift Tax Exclusion.** The Exclusion was $10,000 per person, per year, until 2002, when it was adjusted for inflation to $11,000 and again in 2006 to $12,000 (26 U.S.C. 2503). For most of us, this is not a concern because no federal Estate Tax need be paid unless the decedent's Taxable Estate exceeds the federal **Estate Tax Exclusion** amount.   That value is currently two million dollars and is scheduled to go even higher:

YEAR	ESTATE TAX EXCLUSION AMOUNT
2006-2008	$2,000,000
2009	$3,500,000

Under current law, the federal Estate Tax is scheduled to be phased out in the year 2010, but reinstated once again in the year 2011 with an Exclusion Amount of $1,000,000 — unless lawmakers change the tax law once again.

There is an unlimited marital tax deduction for property transferred to the surviving spouse who is a U.S. citizen; so in most cases, no Estate Tax need be paid if the decedent was married. Regardless of whether taxes are due, federal and state Estate Tax returns must be filed whenever the decedent's Estate exceeds the federal Estate Tax Exclusion Amount in effect as of his date of death. Both state and federal returns are due within nine months of the date of death (26 U.S.C. 6075, ORC 5731.23).

THE OHIO ESTATE TAX

The Personal Representative needs to file an Ohio Estate Tax return if the decedent's Gross Estate exceeds $338,333. The *Gross Estate* includes all of the property he owned, with the exception of his out-of-state property (ORC 5731.01). If Probate is not necessary, whoever takes possession of property subject to the Ohio Estate Tax, is responsible to file the return (ORC 5731.21).

THE TAXABLE ESTATE

As with the federal Estate Tax, there is unlimited marital deduction, so if the decedent is survived by a spouse, no Estate Tax is due on the value of the property inherited by the spouse (ORC 5731.15, 5731.161). The state also allows deductions for funeral expenses, unreimbursed medical expenses, the costs of Probate and charitable donations. See Ohio statute (ORC 5731.16 and 5731.17) for a complete list of deductions.

The decedent's *Taxable Estate* is the value of his Gross Estate, less allowable deductions. Property that is subject to the Ohio Estate Tax rate is taxable at the following rate:

TAXABLE ESTATE	ESTATE TAX
Up to $40,000	2% of the Taxable Estate
Over $40,000 up to $100,000	$800 + 3% of amount over $40,000
Over $100,000 up to $200,000	$2,600 + 4% of amount over $100,000
Over $200,000 up to $300,000	$6,600 + 5% of amount over $200,000
Over $300,000 up to $500,000	$11,600 + 6% of amount over $300,000
Over $500,000	$23,600 + 7% of amount over $500,000

As of June, 2006, Ohio allows a tax credit of $13,900, so that amount can be subtracted from whatever is due (ORC 5731.02).

GETTING OHIO ESTATE TAX CLEARANCE

You have nine months from the decedent's death to file the federal and state Estate Tax (ORC 5731.21). It is a good idea to consult with an accountant or an attorney as soon as practicable after the death so you can make arrangements to pay any tax that may be due.

Another reason to promptly attend to taxes, is that you will need tax clearance before you can get possession of many of the items owned by the decedent. For example, if the decedent held a stock certificate in his name, or jointly with another, the company may refuse to transfer the certificate to the new owner without written consent of the tax commissioner. If the decedent had a joint bank account, the joint owner can withdraw up to 75% of the account but the bank will require tax clearance before they allow the remaining 25% to be withdrawn (ORC 5731.39).

In all other cases, you need the written consent of the tax commissioner before you can get possession of these items. To get permission you need to complete Ohio tax form 12 and Ohio tax form 14, and then file the forms with the Auditor in the county of the decedent's residence. If the decedent did not live in Ohio, you need to complete forms 12A and 14A and file them with the Auditor in the county where the decedent's property is located.

You can get these tax forms by calling (800) 977-7711, or you can download the forms from the Ohio Department of Taxation web site. http://www.tax.ohio.gov/

THE UN-UNIFIED GIFT TAX

As explained, the federal Annual Gift Tax Exclusion was $10,000 up until 2002. It is $12,000 for the year 2006. The IRS keeps a running count of amounts you give to someone that exceed the Annual Gift Tax Exclusion that is in effect in the year of your donation. Although you are required to report a gift that exceeds the Annual Gift Tax Exclusion, no tax needs to be paid unless your running count is more than the federal lifetime Gift Tax Exclusion. That amount is currently one million dollars.

If your running total does not exceed your lifetime Gift Tax Exclusion Amount, once you die, the value of the gifts reported to the IRS will be added to your Taxable Estate for Estate Tax purposes. If you are in that tax bracket, your beneficiaries may need to pay an Estate Tax on gifts made during your lifetime.

Until the Estate Tax law was changed, the Gift and Estate Tax were unified. No Gift Tax needed to be paid unless the total value of the taxable gifts exceeded the federal Estate Tax Exclusion Amount. In 2004 that changed. The Estate Tax Exclusion amount went up to $1,500,000, but the amount for the Gift Tax Exclusion remained at $1,000,000, so they now are no longer unified.

To summarize:
If you make a gift to anyone greater than the Annual Gift Tax Exclusion for that year, you must report the gift to the IRS. The IRS keeps a running count of gifts you made in excess of the Annual Gift Tax Exclusion. You will pay a Gift Tax on gifts given during your lifetime in excess of one million dollars. If the running count does not exceed one million dollars, it is added to your Taxable Estate once you die. The Estate Tax is scheduled to be phased out in 2010, but not the federal Gift Tax. There is no Ohio Gift Tax as of the year 2006.

The current federal Estate Tax is scheduled to be phased out in the year 2010, but a new Capital Gains Tax is scheduled for 2010 that may prove even more costly than the Estate Tax. The new Capital Gains Tax is related to the way inherited property is evaluated by the federal government. Real and personal property is inherited at a "stepped-up" basis, meaning that if the decedent's property increased in value from the time he acquired it, the beneficiary inherits the property at its fair market value as of the decedent's date of death.

For example, if the decedent bought stock for $20,000 and it is worth $50,000 as of his date of death, the beneficiary will take a step-up in basis of $30,000; i.e. the beneficiary inherits the stock at the current $50,000 value. If the beneficiary sells the stock for $50,000, he pays no Capital Gains Tax. If the beneficiary holds onto the stock and later sells it for $60,000, the beneficiary will pay a Capital Gains Tax only on the $10,000 increase in value since the decedent's death.

Up to 2009, there is no limit to the amount a beneficiary can take as a step-up in basis. But in 2010 caps are set in place. The decedent's Estate will be allowed a 1.3 million dollar step-up in basis, plus another 3 million for property passing to the surviving spouse (26 U.S.C. 1022(b)).

The new law could result in significant Capital Gains Taxes that the beneficiary must pay. For example, suppose in 2010 you inherit a business from your father that he purchased for $100,000 and it is now worth 2 million dollars. There is a capital gain of 1.9 million dollars, but you are allowed a step-up in basis of only 1.3 million. If you sell it for 2 million dollars $600,000 of your inheritance will be subject to a Capital Gains Tax.

SPOUSE   SELLING THE HOME

In the tough "ol' days" the IRS allowed *Capital Gains Tax Exclusion* (up to $125,000) on the sale of one's **homestead** (i.e., principal residence). A person had to be 55 or older to take advantage of the Capital Gains Tax Exclusion, and it was a once-in-a-lifetime tax break. If a married couple sold their home and took the Tax Exclusion it was "used up" and no longer available to either partner.

In these, the good times, the IRS allows you to sell your home and up to $250,000 ($500,000 for a married couple) of the profit is free of the Capital Gains Tax. There is no limit to the number of times you can use the Exclusion, provided you own and live in the home at least two of the last five years prior to the sale (26 U.S.C. 121).

If, under the old law, the decedent and his spouse used their "once in a lifetime" Capital Gains Exclusion, with this new law, the surviving spouse can sell the homestead and once again take advantage of the tax break.

BENEFICIARY OF THE
OHIO HOMESTEAD

Those who are permanently and totaled disabled, or 65 or older, and of limited income may be entitled to a reduction in their homestead property taxes, provided they occupy their Ohio home as their primary residence (ORC 323.152). If the decedent's homestead is transferred to a new owner through a sale or inheritance, the County Auditor must be notified of the change of ownership.

If the decedent was receiving a *Homestead Tax Reduction*, the surviving spouse may be entitled to the same reduction provided the spouse is at least 59 when the decedent died. Of course if the surviving spouse, or the new owner of the home is 65 or disabled, he can apply to the County Auditor for his own Homestead Tax Reduction (ORC 323.153).

You can call (888) 644-6778 for information about property taxes including the telephone number and address of the County Auditor, or you can visit the Department of Taxation Web site.

http://www.tax.ohio.gov

Special Situation > DECEDENT WITH A TRUST

A decedent who was the **Settlor** (or *Grantor*) of a Trust, was probably managing the Trust as *Trustee* during his lifetime. The document that sets out the terms of the Trust (the **Trust Agreement)** should name a **Successor Trustee** to manage the Trust property now that the Settlor is deceased. The Agreement may instruct the Successor Trustee to make certain gifts or the Trust document may direct the Successor Trustee to hold money in trust for a beneficiary of the Trust.

 **☎ LAWYER** — IF YOU ARE SUCCESSOR TRUSTEE

If you are the Successor Trustee, in addition to following the terms of the Trust, you are required to obey all of the laws of the state of Ohio relating to the administration of the Trust. For example, if the Trust contains real property, you might need to file an *Affidavit* (a sworn, written statement) with the County Auditor and the County Recorder identifying all Trustees and their current address (ORC 5302.171). You should consult with an attorney experienced in Estate Planning to help you administer the Trust according to the law and without any liability to you.

IF YOU ARE A BENEFICIARY OF THE TRUST

If you are a beneficiary of the Trust, you need to obtain a copy of the Trust to learn how the Trust will be administered now that the Settlor is deceased. Most Trust documents are written in "legalese," so you may want to employ your own attorney to review the Trust, and to explain your rights under the Trust.

NOTIFYING THE BUSINESS COMMUNITY

People and companies who were doing business with the decedent need to be notified of his death. This includes utility companies, credit card companies, banks, brokerage firms and any company that insured the decedent.

NOTIFY CREDIT CARD COMPANIES

You need to notify the decedent's credit card companies of the death. If you can find the contract with the credit card company, check to see whether the decedent had credit card insurance. If the decedent had credit card insurance, then the balance of the account is now paid in full. If you cannot find the contract, contact the company and get a copy of the contract along with a statement of the balance due as of the date of death.

DESTROY DECEDENT'S CREDIT CARDS

You need to destroy all of the decedent's credit cards. If you hold a credit card jointly with the decedent, then it is important to waste no time in closing that account and opening another in your name only.

That's something Barbara knows from hard experience. She and Hank never married but they did live together for several years before he died from liver disease. Hank came from a well to do family so he had enough money to support himself and Barbara during his long illness. Hank put Barbara on all of his credit card accounts so that she could purchase things when he became too ill to go shopping with her. After the funeral, Barbara had a gathering of friends and family at their apartment. Barbara was so preoccupied with her loss that she never noticed that Hank's credit cards were missing until the bills started coming in.

Barbara did not know who ran up the bills on Hank's credit cards during the month following his death. It was obvious that Hank's signature had been forged — but who forged it? One credit card company suspected that it might have been Barbara herself to get out of paying the bill by saying that the card had been stolen

Because the cards were held jointly, Barbara became liable to either pay the charges to the credit card or prove that she did not make the purchases. She was able to clear her credit record but it took several months and she had to employ an attorney to help her do so.

NOTIFY INSURANCE COMPANIES

Examine the decedent's financial records to determine the name and telephone number of all of the companies that insured the decedent or his property. This includes real property insurance, motor vehicle insurance, health insurance and life insurance.

MOTOR VEHICLE INSURANCE

Locate the insurance policy for any type of motor vehicle owed by the decedent (car, truck, boat, airplane) and notify the insurance company of the death. Determine how long insurance coverage continues after the death. Ask the insurance agent to explain what things are covered under the policy. Is the motor vehicle covered for all types of casualty (theft, accident, vandalism, etc.) or is coverage limited in some way?

If you can continue coverage, determine when the next insurance payment is due. Hopefully, the car will be sold or transferred to a beneficiary before that date, but if not, you need to arrange for sufficient insurance coverage during the Probate procedure.

┌───┐

ACCIDENTAL DEATH

If the decedent died as a result of an accident, then check for all possible sources of accident insurance coverage including his homeowner's policy. Some credit card companies provide accident insurance as part of their contract with their card holders. If the decedent died in an automobile accident, check to see whether he was covered by any type of travel insurance, such as rental car insurance. If he belonged to an automobile club, such as AAA, check whether he had accident insurance as part of his club membership.

└───┘

LIFE INSURANCE COMPANIES

If the decedent's life was insured, you need to locate the policy and notify the company of his death. Call each life insurance company and ask what they require in order to forward the insurance proceeds to the beneficiary. Most companies will ask you to send them the original policy and a certified copy of the death certificate. Send the original policy by certified mail or any of the overnight services that require a signed receipt for the package. Make a copy of the original policy for your records before mailing the original policy to the company.

BANK ACCOUNT LIFE INSURANCE

Many banks, credit unions, and savings and loan associations provide life insurance at no cost to the owner of the account. While the amounts are generally small ($1,000 to $5,000), it is insurance that is often overlooked when settling the decedent's affairs. If you do not find a record of such policy, contact each financial institution to determine whether such insurance is offered by the company.

IF YOU CANNOT LOCATE THE POLICY

If you know that the decedent was insured, but you cannot locate the insurance policy, you can contact the company and request a copy of the policy. A tougher question is how to locate the policy if you do not know the name of the insurance company. The American Council of Life Insurers offers suggestions that you may find helpful at the Missing Policy Inquiry page of its Website.

 AMERICAN COUNCIL OF LIFE INSURERS
http://www.acli.com

IF YOU CANNOT LOCATE THE COMPANY

If you cannot locate the insurance company it may be doing business under another name or it may no longer be doing business in the state of Ohio. Each state has a branch of government that regulates insurance companies doing business in that state. If you are having difficulty locating the insurance company, you can call the Department of Insurance in the state where the policy was purchased and ask for assistance in locating the company. In Ohio, you can call the Department of Insurance at (800) 686-1526, or visit their Web site for a list of agents.
http://www.olhioinsurance.gov

EAGLE PUBLISHING COMPANY OF BOCA has the telephone number of the Department of Insurance for each state at the PUBLIC INFORMATION section of its Website.
http://www.eaglepublishing.com

WORK RELATED INSURANCE

If the decedent was employed, check his records for information about work related benefits. He may have survivor benefits from a company or group life insurance plan and/or a retirement plan. Also check with the employer about company benefits. If the decedent belonged to a union, ask the employer who you can contact to determine whether there are any union benefits.

The decedent may have belonged to a professional, fraternal or social organization such as the local Chamber of Commerce, a Veteran's organization, the Kiwanis, AARP, the Rotary Club, etc. If he belonged to any such organization, check to see whether the organization provided any type of insurance coverage.

Special Situation ▷ BUSINESS OWNED BY DECEDENT

If the decedent owned his own company or was a partner in a company, he may have purchased "key man" insurance. Key man insurance is a policy designed to protect the company should a valuable employee become disabled or die. Benefits are paid to the company to compensate the company for the loss of someone who is essential to the continuation of the business. Ultimately the policy benefits those who inherit the business.

If the decedent had an ownership interest in an ongoing business (sole proprietor, shareholder or partner), there may be a shareholder's or partnership agreement requiring the company to purchase the decedent's share of the business. The Personal Representative or his attorney needs to investigate to see if there was a key man insurance policy and/or such purchase agreement.

CORPORATE OWNER OR STATUTORY AGENT

If the decedent was the sole owner and officer of a corporation , the Ohio Secretary of State needs to be notified of the change of ownership. There may need to be a Probate proceeding in order to transfer ownership of the company to the proper beneficiary, so it may take some time before new officers and directors are identified.

Ohio law requires each corporation to continuously maintain a *Statutory Agent* who lives in the state. If the decedent was the Statutory Agent of the company, a new Agent must be appointed as soon as is practicable (ORC 1701.07 (D)). You can get forms to change officers, directors and Statutory Agent by calling the OHIO OFFICE OF THE SECRETARY OF STATE, Business Services Division at (877) 767-3453 or by writing to:

Ohio Secretary of State
Business Services Division
30 Broad Street, 14th Floor
Columbus, OH   43266-0418

STATUS REPORT
If you were not actively involved in running the business, you might request a status report of the company. The report will show whether filing fees are current and will identify the officers and directors of the company. The Ohio Secretary of State has a Web site from which you can download forms and obtain information about Ohio corporations.

OHIO SECRETARY OF STATE
http://ohio.gov/sos/

HOMEOWNER'S INSURANCE

If the decedent owned his own home, then check whether there is sufficient insurance coverage on the property. The decedent may have neglected to increase his insurance as the property appreciated in value. If you think the property may be vacant for some period of time, then it is important to have vandalism coverage included in the policy. Once the property is sold, or transferred to the proper beneficiary, you can have the policy discontinued or transferred to the new owner. The decedent's Estate should receive a refund for the unused portion of the premium.

MORTGAGE INSURANCE

If the decedent had a mortgage on any parcel of real estate that he owned, he might have arranged with his lender for an insurance policy that pays off the mortgage balance in the event of his death. Look at the closing statement to see whether there was a charge for mortgage insurance. Also check with the lender to determine if such a policy was purchased.

If there was no mortgage insurance, and the decedent was the sole owner, the beneficiary of the property needs to make arrangements with the lender to continue making payments on the mortgage or to refinance the loan.

NOTIFY THE HOMEOWNERS ASSOCIATION

If the decedent owned a condominium or a residence regulated by a homeowners association, the association will need to be notified of the change of ownership. Once the property is transferred, the new owner will need to contact the association to learn of the rules and regulations of the association. The new owner will need to arrange to have notices of dues and assessments forwarded to him.

HEALTH INSURANCE

You need to determine whether the decedent had health insurance, and if so, you should locate the original policy. If you know he had insurance, but cannot find the policy, have the insurance company send you a copy. The decedent's insurance carrier probably knows of the death, but it is a good idea to contact them to report the death and to verify that the medical treatment given before his death is covered by the policy.

 *Special Situation*   DECEDENT ON MEDICARE

If the decedent was covered by Medicare, you do not need to notify anyone, but you do need to know what things were covered by Medicare so that you can determine what medical bills are (or are not) covered by Medicare. The government publication **MEDICARE AND YOU** (Publication No. CMS-10050) explains what things are covered under Medicare and the different kinds of plans that are currently available. You can get the publication by writing to:

U.S. Dept. of Health and Human Services
Centers for Medicare and Medicaid Services
7500 Security Boulevard
Baltimore, MD 21244-1850

You can download the publication from the Internet.

 MEDICARE WEB SITE
http://www.medicare.gov

The publication is available on Audiotape, in Braille, in large print and in Spanish. To receive a copy you can call (800) 633-4227. TTY users call (877) 486-2048.

If the surviving spouse is insured under Medicare, the decedent's death does not affect the spouse's coverage. If the surviving spouse has her own health insurance plan that also covered the decedent, the spouse needs to notify the employer of the death because this may affect the cost of the plan to the employer and/or the surviving spouse. If the spouse was covered under the decedent's policy, (s)he needs to arrange for new coverage. There are state and federal laws that ensure continued coverage under the decedent's health insurance plan for a period of time depending on whether the decedent's employer falls under federal or state regulation.

If the decedent was employed by a federally regulated company (usually a company with at least twenty employees), under the Consolidated Omnibus Budget Reconciliation Act ("COBRA") the employer must make the company health plan available to the surviving spouse and any dependent child of the decedent for up to 36 months. The employer is required to give notice to the surviving spouse that the spouse and/or dependent child have the right to continue coverage under the decedent's health plan. The spouse and/or child have 60 days from the date of death or 60 days after the employer sends notice (whichever is later) to tell the employer whether the surviving spouse and child wish to continue with the health insurance plan (29 U.S.C. Sec. 1162, 1163, 1165).

CAUTION NO GRACE PERIOD FOR PAYMENT

Health Insurance premiums must be paid on or before each due date. If you wish continued coverage, you need to make that payment when it comes due.

SPOUSE'S HEALTH INSURANCE (continued)

A problem with continued coverage may be the cost. Before the death, the employer may have been paying some percentage of the premium. The employer has no such duty after the death unless there was some employment agreement stating otherwise. Under COBRA, the employer may charge the spouse for the full cost of the plan plus a 2% administrative fee.

If you have a question about continued coverage under COBRA, call the EMPLOYEE BENEFIT SECURITY ADMINISTRATION toll free at (866) 444-3272 and ask for their latest publication, or you can visit the HEALTH PLAN AND BENEFITS section of the U.S. Department of Labor Web site for information about COBRA.

 U.S. DEPARTMENT OF LABOR
http://www.dol.gov/

HEALTH INSURANCE COVERAGE UNDER OHIO LAW

Under Ohio law, all individual (i.e., non-group) sickness and accident insurance policies must contain a provision that family members who were covered by the decedent's policy have the right to continue coverage. Coverage may be continued through the issuance of a converted or separate policy, provided the terms of the policy are not less favorable than coverage under the decedent's policy. To continue coverage the family members must notify the insurer and make payment of the premium within 31 days following the death (ORC 3923.32). For information about continued health care insurance, call the OHIO DEPARTMENT OF INSURANCE Consumer Hotline at (800) 686-1526 or visit the Consumer Services section of the Ohio Department of Insurance Web site.

 THE OHIO DEPARTMENT OF INSURANCE
http://www.ohioinsurance.gov

Probably the last person in the world to learn of the decedent's death is the direct mail advertiser. Advertisers are nothing if not tenacious. It is not uncommon for advertisements to be mailed to the decedent for more than ten years after the death. It is not because the advertiser is trying to sell something to the decedent, but rather the people who prepare (and sell) mailing lists do not know that he is dead.

Those who sell mailing lists may not be motivated to update the list because of the cost of doing the necessary research; and perhaps because the price of the mailing list is often based on the number of people on the list. Even those who compose their own list may decide it is less costly to mail to everyone, than take the time (and money) to update the list.

If it gives you pleasure to think of advertisers spending substantial sums for nothing, then that is what you should do (nothing). But for those of you who wince each time you see another piece of mail addressed to the decedent, you can have the Direct Marketing Association place the name of the decedent on their Deceased Do-Not-Contact List. You can do this by registering the decedent's name, address, phone number and e-mail address at the Direct Marketing Association Web site. There is a $1 credit card verification fee. The fee is made so that the Direct Marketing Association has a record of who registered the decedent's name.

 THE DIRECT MARKETING ASSOCIATION
http://www.the-dma.org

Once registered, members of the Direct Marketing Association are required to remove the decedent's name from their contact list.

✍ CHANGE BENEFICIARIES ✍

If the decedent was someone you named as beneficiary of your insurance policy, Will, Trust, brokerage account or pension plan, then you may need to name another beneficiary in his place:

INSURANCE POLICY ✍

If you named the decedent as the primary beneficiary of your life insurance policy, check to see whether you named a contingent (alternate) beneficiary in the event that the decedent did not survive you. If not, you need to contact the insurance company and name a new beneficiary. If you did name a contingent beneficiary, that person is now your primary beneficiary and you need to consider whether you wish to name a new contingent beneficiary at this time.

HEALTH INSURANCE POLICY ✍

If the decedent was covered under your health insurance policy, your employer and the health insurer need to be notified of the death because this may affect the cost of the plan to you and/or your employer.

WILL OR TRUST ✍

Most Wills provide for a contingent beneficiary in the event that the person named as beneficiary dies first. If you named the decedent as your beneficiary, check to see whether you named an alternate beneficiary. If not, you need to have your attorney revise your Will and name a new beneficiary.

Similarly, if you are the Settlor of a Trust and the decedent was one of the beneficiaries of your Trust, check the Trust document to see if you named an alternate beneficiary. If not, contact your attorney to prepare an amendment to the Trust, naming a new beneficiary.

BANK AND SECURITIES ACCOUNTS ✍

If the decedent was a beneficiary or joint owner of your bank or securities account, you may wish to arrange for a new beneficiary or joint owner at this time.

PENSION PLANS ✍

If the decedent was a beneficiary under your pension plan, you need to notify them of the death and name a new beneficiary. Many pension plans require that you notify them within a set period of time (usually 30 days from the date of death), so it is important to notify them as soon as you are able. If the decedent was a beneficiary of your Individual Retirement Account ("IRA") or of your Qualified Retirement Plan ("QRP") and you did not provide for an alternate beneficiary, you need to name another beneficiary.

Before you choose an alternate beneficiary, it is important that you understand all of the options available to you. Not an easy task. There are many complex government regulations relating to IRA and QRP accounts. Even if you believe you understood your options when you set up your account, the federal government often changes those options.

Your choice of beneficiary might impact the amount of money you can withdraw each month, so it is important to consult with your accountant, tax attorney or financial planner, before you make your election.

NOTIFYING CREDITORS

It is the job of the person appointed as Personal Representative to notify the decedent's creditors of the death so that creditors are given an opportunity to come forward and file a *claim* (a written demand for payment) for monies owed. The attorney for the Personal Representative usually takes care of the notice procedure. We will explain that procedure later in this book.

If Probate is not necessary, the next of kin can notify the creditors of the death, but before doing so, it is important to read Chapter 4: WHAT BILLS NEED TO BE PAID? That chapter explains what bills need to be paid and who is responsible to pay them.

Before any bill can be paid, you need to know whether the decedent left any asset that can be used to pay those debts. The next chapter explains how to identify, and then locate, all of the property owned by the decedent.

Locating the Assets 3

It is important to locate the financial records of the decedent and then carefully examine those records. Even the partner in a long-term marriage should conduct a thorough search because the surviving spouse may be unaware of all that was owned (or owed) by the decedent.

It is not unusual for a surviving spouse to be surprised when learning of the decedent's business transactions, especially in those cases where the decedent had control of family finances. One such example is that of Sam and Henrietta. They married just as soon as Sam was discharged from the army. During their marriage, Sam handled all of the finances, giving Henrietta just enough money to run the household.

Every now and again, Henrietta would think of getting a job. She longed to have her own source of income and some economic independence. Each time she brought up the subject Sam would loudly object. He had no patience for this modern wife thing. He got married to have a real wife — one who would cook his meals and keep house for him. He reminded her that the reason they married was because they shared these family values.

Henrietta was not the arguing type. She rationalized, saying that Sam had a delicate stomach and dust allergies. He needed her to prepare his special meals and keep an immaculate house for him. Besides, Sam had a good job with a major cruise line and he needed her to accompany him on his frequent business trips.

Once Sam retired, he was even more cautious in his spending habits. Henrietta seldom complained. She assumed the reason for his "thrift" was that they had little money and had to live on his pension.

They were married 52 years when Sam died at the age of 83. Henrietta was 81 at the time of his death. She was one very happy, very angry and very aged widow when she discovered that Sam left her with assets worth well over a million dollars!

LOCATING RECORDS

As you go through the papers of the decedent you may come across documents that indicate property ownership, such as bank registers, stock or bond certificates, insurance policies, pension or annuity records, etc. Place all evidence of ownership in a single place. You will need to contact the different companies in order to transfer title to the proper beneficiary.

To obtain the property, you may need to produce evidence of the decedent's personal relationships, such as a marriage or birth certificate, or naturalization papers, or military personnel records. If you cannot locate the decedent's marriage or birth certificate, you can get a copy of those records from the Vital Statistics office in the state where the event took place. Many states restrict access to these records to the decedent's Personal Representative or to close family members. You can use the Internet to locate Vital Statistics by using your favorite search engine to find Vital Statistics or Vital Records in the given state.

MILITARY RECORDS
The next of kin can obtain a copy of the military record of a deceased veteran by writing to:

The National Personnel Records Center
Military Personnel Records
9700 Page Avenue
St. Louis, MO   63132-5100

They will send you form SF 180 to complete. You can fax your request to them at (314) 801-9195, or you can download the form from the Internet.

 National Archives and Records Administration
http://www.vetrecs.archives.gov

COLLECT AND IDENTIFY KEYS

The decedent may have kept his records in a safe deposit box, so you may find that your first job is to locate the keys to the box. As you go through the personal effects of the decedent, collect and identify all the keys that you find. If you come across an unidentified key, it could be a key to a post office box (private or federal) or a safe deposit box located in a bank or in a private vault company. You will need to determine whether that key opens a box that contains property belonging to the decedent or whether the key is to a box no longer in use. Some ways to investigate are as follows:

☑ CHECK BUSINESS RECORDS

If the decedent kept receipts, look through those items to see if he paid for the rental of a post office or safe deposit box. Also, look at his check register to see if he wrote a check to the Postmaster or to any safe deposit or vault company. Look at his bank statements to see if there is any bank charge for a safe deposit box. Some banks bill separately for safe deposit boxes so check with all of the banks in which the decedent had an account to determine if he had a safe deposit box with that bank.

☑ CHECK THE KEY TYPE

If you cannot identify the key, take it to a local locksmith and ask whether anyone can identify the type of facility that uses such keys. If that doesn't work, go to each bank, post office and private safe deposit box company where the decedent shopped, worked or frequented and ask whether they use the type of key that you found.

☑ CHECK THE MAIL

Check the mail over the next several months to see if the decedent receives a statement requesting payment for the next year's rental of a post office or safe deposit box.

FORWARD THE DECEDENT'S MAIL

You may find evidence of a brokerage account, bank account, or safe deposit box by examining correspondence addressed to the decedent. If he was living alone, have his mail forwarded to the person he named as Personal Representative or Executor of his Will. If the decedent did not leave a Will, and Probate is not necessary, forward the mail to his next of kin. Call the Postmaster and ask him to send you the necessary forms to make the change. Request that the mail be forwarded for the longest period allowed by law (currently one year).

Instead of calling, you can download the change of address form from the U.S. Postal Service Web site.

U.S. POSTAL SERVICE
http://www.usps.com

THE POST OFFICE BOX RENTAL
The decedent may have been renting a post office box at his local post office branch or perhaps at the branch closest to where he did his banking. Ask the Postmaster to help you determine whether the decedent was renting a post office box. If so, you need to locate the key to the box so that you can collect the decedent's mail.

LOST POST OFFICE BOX KEY
If the decedent had a post office box and you cannot locate the key, contact the postmaster and ask him to give you the necessary forms to complete in order to get possession of the mail in that box.

As before, have all mail addressed to that box forwarded to the Personal Representative, or if Probate is not necessary, to the decedent's next of kin.

WHAT TO DO WITH CHECKS

You may receive checks in the mail made out to the decedent. Social Security checks, pension checks and annuity checks issued after the date of death may need to be returned to the sender (see pages 32 and 34 of this book). Other checks need to be deposited. If Probate is necessary, the Personal Representative will open a Probate Estate account and deposit the decedent's checks to that account.

If Probate is not necessary, checks can be deposited to any account held in the name of the decedent. The decedent is not here to endorse the check, but you can deposit it to his account by writing his bank account number on the back of the check and printing beneath it **FOR DEPOSIT ONLY.**

The bank will accept such an endorsement and deposit the check into the decedent's account. The account can then be transferred to the proper beneficiary using an appropriate transfer procedure as described later in Chapter 6.

If the check is significant in value or the decedent had different accounts that are accessible to different people, then there needs to be cooperation and a sense of fair play. If not, the dollar gain may not nearly offset the emotional turmoil. That was the case with Gail. Her father made her a joint owner of his checking account to assist in paying his bills. He had macular degeneration and it was increasingly difficult for him to see. He also had a savings account that was in his name only.

Gail's brother Ken had a good paying job in Hawaii. Even though he lived at a distance, Ken, his wife and two children always spent the Christmas holidays with his father and sister.

Each winter, their father enjoyed leaving the cold of Ohio to spend a few weeks enjoying the warm Hawaii sunshine.

One winter the father purchased a round trip ticket to Hawaii. It cost several hundred dollars. Just before the departure date, the father had a heart attack and died. Gail called the airline to cancel the ticket. They refunded the money in a check made out to her father. She deposited the check to the joint account, and then closed it out.

As part of the Probate procedure, the money in the father's savings account was transferred to the Probate Estate account and then divided equally between Ken and his sister. Ken wondered what happened to the money from the airline tickets.

Gail explained "Dad paid for the tickets from the joint account, so I deposited the money back to that account. "

"Aren't you going to give me half?"

"Dad meant for me to have whatever was in that joint account. If he wanted you to have half of the money, he would have made you joint owner as well."

Ken didn't see it that way "That refund was part of Dad's Probate Estate. It should have been deposited to the Probate Estate account and then divided equally between us. Are you going to force me to argue this in Court?"

Gail finally agreed to split the money with Ken, but the damage was done.

Gail complains that holidays are lonely since Dad died.

LOCATE FINANCIAL RECORDS

To locate the decedent's assets you need to find evidence of what he owned and where those assets are located. As you go through the papers of the decedent you should find documents that indicate property ownership, such as deeds, bank registers, title to motor vehicles, insurance policies, stock or bond certificates, etc. You will need these documents in order to transfer title to the proper beneficiary.

Many people keep their financial records in a single place but it is important to check the entire house to be sure you did not miss something.

CHECK THE COMPUTER
Don't overlook that computer sitting silently in the corner. It may hold the decedent's check register and all of his financial records. You may want to monitor his E-mail for E-bank or on-line credit card accounts. The computer may be programmed to protect this information. If you cannot access the decedent's financial records, you may need to employ a computer technician or computer consultant who will be able to print out all of the information on the hard drive of the computer. You can find such a technician or consultant by looking in the telephone book under COMPUTER SUPPORT SERVICES or COMPUTER SYSTEM DESIGNS & CONSULTANTS.

LOCATE OUT OF STATE ACCOUNTS
If the decedent had an out of state bank or a brokerage account, you can locate it through the monthly or quarterly statements mailed to the decedent. All companies are required to send out IRS tax form 1099 each year stating the amount of interest or income earned on an account. Once the forms come in, you will learn the location of all of the decedent's active and inactive (i.e., closed) accounts.

LOCATE TITLE TO MOTOR VEHICLE

You will need the decedent's certificate of title in order to transfer his car to the proper beneficiary (ORC 4505.03). In Ohio, if monies are owed on a motor vehicle (car, mobile home or trailer), the lender takes possession of the original certificate of title until the loan is paid. If you cannot find the original *Certificate of Title*, the lienholder has the original title or it could be that the decedent had an *Ohio Electronic Title*. If so, he will not have a printed title. If you are the surviving owner, or Personal Representative, you can go to the county of the decedent's residence and complete a title request form, giving the title history of the car; or you can write to the OHIO BUREAU OF MOTOR VEHICLES.   Ohio BMV, Title Division
P.O. Box 16520
Columbus, OH   43216

You will need to give them the year and make of the car and its vehicle identification number. If you find there is a loan on the car, contact the lienholder and get a copy of the contract that is the basis of the loan.

THE LEASED CAR

You may find that the car is leased and not owned by the decedent. If so, contact the lessor and get a copy of the lease agreement. Check to see whether the decedent had life insurance as part of the agreement. If he did, the lease may now be paid in full and the beneficiary of the car should be able to use the car for the remainder of the leasing period, or take title to the car, whichever option is available under the lease agreement. If the lease is not paid in full upon the decedent's death, arrangements need to be made to satisfy the terms of the agreement. See Chapter 6 for information about transferring a leased car.

The Clerk of the Court of Common Pleas issues certificates of title (ORC 4505.06). If Probate is necessary, whoever is appointed as Personal Representative will have authority to obtain a duplicate title from the Clerk of the Court of Common Pleas.

NEW TITLE V. DUPLICATE TITLE

If the decedent owned his car jointly with right of survivorship, or if the Certificate of Title indicates that the car is to be transferred to a named beneficiary upon his death, the surviving joint owner or beneficiary can obtain his own title rather than just have a duplicate title issued in the decedent's name (ORC 2131.12, 2131.13).

As we will see in Chapters 4 and 5, the surviving spouse has certain rights in the decedent's car, motor cycle and motor boat. If title to the car (or boat) is in the decedent's name only, the surviving spouse may be able to have the car transferred to his/her name. See Chapter 6 for a discussion of how to transfer title to the decedent's motor vehicle to the surviving spouse.

 THE OUT OF STATE CAR

If the decedent was not a resident of Ohio, he may have a car that is titled and registered in another state. You can get information about titling laws in that state from the AMERICAN ASSOCIATION OF MOTOR VEHICLE Web site.

 AMERICAN ASSOCIATION OF
MOTOR VEHICLE ASSOCIATIONS
http://www.aamva.org

LOCATE TITLE TO SNOWMOBILES/ALL-PURPOSE VEHICLES

All snowmobiles, off-highway motorcycles, and all-purpose vehicles owned, must be titled and registered the same as any other motor vehicle — with the exception of vehicles operated exclusively on the owner's land (ORC 4519.02, 4519.03). An *all-purpose vehicle* is any self-propelled vehicle designed for cross-country travel. This includes mini-bikes, trail bikes and all-terrain vehicles (ORC 4519.01). If the decedent owned one of these vehicles and you cannot locate a Certificate of Title, you can get a duplicate title in the same manner as explained on the previous page.

LOCATE TITLE TO BOAT

With the exception of vessels that are registered with the U.S. Coast Guard, motor boats used primarily in the state of Ohio must be titled with the Clerk in the Title Office of the Court of Common Pleas. If the decedent owned a boat that he used principally in the state of Ohio you should be able to locate its Certificate of Title. The decedent may have opted to use the automated title system and not be issued a physical certificate (ORC 1548.021). If you cannot locate the title, check with the Clerk of the Court of Common Pleas in the county of the decedent's residence to verify that the decedent is the owner of the boat.

In addition to the title, you should find the decedent's Ohio *Registration Certificate* The Registration Certificate is a wallet sized plastic card. Watercraft are registered with the **OHIO DEPARTMENT OF NATURAL RESOURCES**, (ORC 1547.531). If you have a question about the registration of the boat, copy the Hull Identification Number and call the Department of Natural Resources at their toll free number (877) 446-2837. Out of town, call (614) 265-6480.

A *motor home* is a self-propelled recreational vehicle (ORC 4501.01(Q)). It is not permanently attached to real property and is considered to be personal property. It is titled and registered in the same manner as any other motor vehicle. A *mobile home* is a building unit more than 35 feet long. It is built on a permanent chassis (i.e., supporting frame) and is transportable in one or more sections (ORC 4501.01 (O)). Like the mobile home, a *manufactured home* is a structure that is built on a permanent chassis, that is transportable in one or more sections.

A mobile or manufactured home that is permanently affixed to the land does not need to be registered with the Bureau of Motor Vehicles, however, it should be registered with County Auditor in the county where the home is located (ORC 4503.061).

If the decedent's mobile/manufactured home was taxed as real property, he probably turned in his *Certificate of Title*, or *Memorandum of Certificate of Title* to the County Auditor. Once the Auditor places a home on the tax list, he delivers the Certificate to the Clerk of the Court of Common Pleas — who in turn makes the Certificate inactive (ORC 4503.06). If you cannot find any document indicating the decedent's ownership of the mobile/manufactured home, you can ask the Clerk or the County Auditor for a copy of the Certificate of Title.

If the decedent kept his mobile/manufactured home in a leased space, you also need to locate the lease to the lot. If you cannot locate the lease, contact the landlord for a copy, and proceed in the same manner as for a residential lease, as discussed later in this Chapter.

LOCATE TITLE TO AIRCRAFT

If the decedent owned an aircraft, you should find a certificate of title to the aircraft. The Aircraft Registration Branch of the Federal Aviation Administration ("FAA") maintains aircraft records. The Aircraft Registration Branch is located in Oklahoma City, Oklahoma. Aircraft records are open to the general public, but researching the documents yourself may be difficult because the records are maintained by the registration number of the aircraft, and the Aircraft Registration Branch does not furnish lien information or the names of previous owners.

The Aircraft Registration Branch does not perform title searches, however they can give you a list of title search companies. You can call them toll free at (866) 835-5322, or visit their Website for a list of title companies.

 THE FEDERAL AVIATION ADMINISTRATION
http://www.faa.gov/

In addition to locating title to the aircraft, you should find a *Certificate of Registration* within the aircraft. Ohio statute requires that all aircraft be registered with the Ohio Director of Transportation (ORC 4561.19).

If you have a question about the registration of the airplane, call the Department of Transportation at (614) 387-2354.

See Chapter 6 for an explanation of how the beneficiary of the aircraft can obtain his own Certificate of Registration.

If the decedent was renting his residence, he may have a written lease agreement. It is important to locate the lease because the decedent's Estate may be responsible for payments under the lease. If you cannot find a lease, ask the landlord for a copy. If he reports that there was no written lease, verify that the decedent was on a month to month basis and then work out a mutually agreeable time in which to vacate the premises.

If a written lease is in effect, determine the end of the lease period, and whether the landlord is holding a security deposit. Ask whether he will agree to cancel the lease on condition that the property is promptly vacated and left in good condition. If the landlord wants to hold the Estate responsible to pay the balance of the lease, have your attorney review the lease to determine what rights and responsibilities remain now that the tenant is deceased.

☎ LAWYER   DECEDENT'S ONGOING BUSINESS

If the decedent was the sole owner of a business, or if he owned a partnership interest in a business, the Personal Representative needs to take possession of the decedent's business records and make arrangements for the continued operation of the business (ORC 2113.30). The company accountant or lawyer may be able to assist in obtaining the records. If you are a beneficiary of the Estate, consider consulting with your own attorney to determine what rights and responsibilities you may have in the business.

COLLECT DEEDS

Collect deeds to all of the *real property* (lot, residential property, condominium) owned by the decedent. If the decedent acquired the property either as a beneficiary under a Will or according to the Ohio Laws of Descent, you should find a *Certificate of Transfer* identifying the decedent as the owner of the property he inherited (ORC 2113.61).

In addition to the deed, look for other documents associated with the property, such as a mortgage. You may come across a title insurance policy. The new owner might be able to turn in that policy and receive a discount toward the purchase of a new title insurance, so it is important to keep the policy together with the deed. Instead of a title insurance policy you may find an *Abstract of Title*. An Abstract of Title is a summary of the documents or facts appearing on the public record which affect title to the property. The Abstract will need to be updated once the property is transferred.

THE TORRENS SYSTEM

The state Ohio has a dual system for keeping records of the ownership of real property. Deeds to real property are recorded in the office of County Recorder in the county where the property is located. This is the way most deeds are recorded. However, some counties also use the *Torrens System* for establishing title to real property. Under the Torrens System, the property is registered with the Court of Common Pleas or the Probate Court in the county where the property is located (ORC 5309.02). Upon application by the owner of the property, or his attorney, the Court will examine title to the property, and then issue a *Certificate of Title* in the owner's name (ORC 5309.05).

If the decedent's real property was registered under the Torrens System, you should find a Certificate of Title instead of a deed.

In 1991, the legislature passed statutes allowing counties to abolish the Torrens System within their county. If the decedent's property is registered in a county that abolished the Torrens System, the property will be transferred to the new owner by deed or by Certificate of Transfer.

THE CONDOMINIUM

The decedent may have owned a condominium. A condominium is a system of individual units. Each owner of the unit has a right to common areas in the building. You should find a deed to the unit, a recorded *Condominium Approval* of the transfer of the condominium to the decedent, and a copy of the *condominium documents* that regulate the complex. If the decedent owned a condominium and you cannot locate the condominium documents, contact the Condominium Association, or its management company to get a copy of the documents.

THE LOST DEED

If you know that the decedent owned real property, but you cannot find the deed, contact the County Recorder in the county where the property is located. He should be able to provide you with a copy of the last recorded deed.

CHECK FOR MINERAL RIGHTS

You may find documents associated with rights to real property, such as oil, gas, coal and other mineral rights. These rights may be in the form of royalty interests in the land. Check the decedent's last three income tax returns to determine whether he included mineral royalty payments as part of his income.

You need to locate the deed and any related document (Abstract of Title, title insurance policy, recorded condominium approval, etc.) to out of state property owned by the decedent. If you know the decedent owned out of state real property, but cannot find the deed, you can use the same procedure just described, namely, you can check with the recording department in the county where the property is located. In Ohio, the County Recorder is in charge of the recording department. In other states, it may be the Clerk of the Circuit Court or the Registrar of Deeds. The Clerk in the recording department should be able to give you a copy of the last recorded deed.

Many states index the property by the name of the current owner of the property, so if you know the county where the property is located, you should be able to find the deed by giving the decedent's name to the Clerk. If you do not know the county in which the property is located, you will need to wait for the next tax bill. The tax bill contains its legal description, or tax identification number.

COLLECT TAX RECORDS

The decedent's final federal income tax return needs to be filed. To prepare the return you may need to refer to the returns he filed over the past three years. If you cannot locate his prior tax records, check his personal telephone book and/or his personal bank register to see if he employed someone to prepare his taxes. His tax preparer should have a copy of those records.

If you are unable to locate the decedent's federal tax returns, they can be obtained from the IRS. The IRS will send copies of the decedent's tax filings to anyone who has a *fiduciary relationship* with the decedent. The IRS considers the following people to be a fiduciary:

➤ the person appointed as the Personal Representative of the decedent's Estate

➤ the Successor Trustee of the decedent's Trust

➤ if the person died without a Will, whoever is legally entitled to possession of the decedent's property. See Chapter 5 for an explanation of the Laws of Descent and Distribution.

The fiduciary can receive copies of the decedent's tax filings by notifying IRS that he is acting in a fiduciary capacity, and then requesting the copies. To notify the IRS of the fiduciary capacity, file Form 56:
NOTICE CONCERNING FIDUCIARY RELATIONSHIP

To request a copy of the tax return, file Form 4506:
REQUEST FOR A COPY OF TAX RETURN

Your accountant can file these forms for you or you can obtain the forms from the IRS by calling (800) 829-3676 or download them from the FORMS section of the IRS Web site.

INTERNAL REVENUE SERVICE
http://www.irs.gov

LOCATE OHIO INCOME TAX RETURN

Ohio Income Taxes are imposed on anyone who lived or earned income within the state (ORC 5747.01). The Personal Representative, or if Probate is not necessary, whoever is entitled to possession of the decedent's property needs to file the state income tax return at the same time the federal income tax return is filed (ORC 5747.08).

You may need last year's return to help prepare the final return. Whoever is responsible to file the return can request a copy by writing to:

OHIO DEPARTMENT OF TAXATION
Attention Taxpayers Services
P.O. Box 182382
Columbus, OH 43218

Before writing, you may want to call the Department of Taxation at (800) 282-1780 and ask what information or document they require in order for you to obtain a copy of the return.

FINDING LOST OR UNCLAIMED PROPERTY

If the decedent was forgetful, he may have money in a lost bank account or abandoned safe deposit box. Property that is unclaimed is turned over to the **OHIO DIRECTOR OF COMMERCE** after a period of time as set by Ohio law. The time period depends on the item:.

- 3 years for unclaimed wages in excess of $50
- 1 year after service is discontinued for an unclaimed utility deposit
- 3 years after monies are payable under a life insurance policy or annuity
- 5 years for a Certificate of Deposit, check or last transaction on a bank account
- 3 years from the expiration of the lease or rental of a safe deposit box
- 15 years from the date of issue of a travelers check

See Ohio statute (ORC 169.02) for a list of items and their time periods.

Before turning the property over to the state, the holder of the unclaimed property must make a good faith effort to contact the owner and return the property to the owner (ORC 169.03). The Superintendent of the Division of Unclaimed Funds is appointed by the Director of Commerce to administer the Ohio unclaimed funds property. He will also try to locate the owner of the unclaimed property by publishing notice in a paper of general circulation giving the name and last known address of the owner of the property (ORC 169.06).

If a tangible item (such as jewelry) remains unclaimed, the Superintendent will convert it to cash by holding a public auction. If the owner (or his heirs) later claims the item, he will receive the net proceeds of the sale.

As of mid 2006, the Superintendent reports that there is more than 2.6 million unclaimed accounts, worth more than $700,000,000 waiting to be returned to their rightful owner.

You can determine whether there is a record identifying the decedent as the owner of unclaimed property by calling (614) 466-4433 or by writing to:

Department of Commerce
Division of Unclaimed Funds
77 South High Street-20th floor
Columbus, OH   43215-6108

You can also get information and download application forms the Ohio Department of Commerce Web site.

 OHIO DEPARTMENT OF COMMERCE
UNCLAIMED FUNDS DIVISION
http://www.com.state.oh.us/unfd

CLAIMS IN OTHER STATES
Each state has an agency or department that is responsible for handling lost, abandoned or unclaimed property located within that state. If the decedent lived in states other than Ohio, you can use the link at the Ohio Division of Unclaimed Funds Web to search for unclaimed property in other states.

CLAIMS FOR DECEDENT VICTIMS OF HOLOCAUST
The New York State Banking Department has a special Claims Processing Office for Holocaust survivors or their heirs. The office processes claims for Swiss bank accounts that were dormant since the end of World War II. If the decedent was a victim of the Holocaust, you can get information about money that may be due to the decedent's Estate by calling (800) 695-3318.

CLAIMS FOR INCOME TAX REFUNDS

The IRS reports that each year they are unable to deliver thousands of income tax refund checks, mostly because a taxpayer moves and neglects to notify the IRS, or the U.S. Postal Service of their new address. In addition to undeliverable income tax refunds, many people are entitled to a refund but no check is sent because they fail to file an income tax return. This is often the case with employees who earned too little income to file a tax return. They may not be aware that taxes withheld from their wages are refundable. Other employees may not have had any tax withheld, but if they had a low income they might be eligible for an Earned Income Tax Credit, provided they file an income tax return. The IRS gives taxpayers three years to claim these funds. There is no penalty for filing a late return in order to qualify for these refunds.

You can determine whether the decedent is entitled to an income tax refund or a Earned Income Tax Credit by calling the IRS at (800) 829-1040. You can also get information about unclaimed tax refunds by visiting the IRS Website.
http://www.irs.gov/

UNCLAIMED OHIO TAX REFUNDS
The Ohio Department of Taxation also reports that thousands of tax refunds are returned to them each year by the U.S. Postal Service marked "undeliverable." You can call the Department of Taxation at (800) 282-1784 to determine whether there is an unclaimed check for the decedent.

You can also check for an unclaimed income tax refund at the Department of Taxation Web site.
http://www.tax.ohio.gov

THE LOST PENSION

The decedent may be entitled to benefits under a pension plan of a prior employer. If the decedent worked for an employer for any significant period of time, say five years or more, check with the company benefit representative to determine whether any pension funds are owed to the decedent. If you are unable to locate the former employer, it could be that the company moved or merged with another company. There are several ways to track down the company, starting with the Ohio Secretary of State, to learn of the company's current status (see page 51).

CONTACT THE UNION
If the decedent belonged to a union, contact them and ask them to help you locate the company. They may be able to tell you whether the company is still in business, and if not, what happened to the company's pension funds.

CONTACT SOCIAL SECURITY
The Social Security Administration has the decedent's work record and the employer identification number for each of his employers. The Personal Representative can get this information by calling the Social Security Administration at (800) 772-1213.

RESEARCH THE INTERNET
Pension Benefit Guaranty Corporation insures private sector pensions. They operate an on-line search tool for those employees who did not collect their pension because the company became bankrupt or dissolved the plan, or because the company could not locate the employee. You can search their Website by employee name or by the company name.

 PENSION BENEFIT GUARANTY CORPORATION
http://www.pbgc.gov/

LOCATE CONTRACTS

HEALTH CLUB CONTRACT

If the decedent belonged to a health club or gym, he may have prepaid for the year. Look for the club contract. It will give the terms of the agreement. If you cannot locate the contract, then contact the company for a copy of the agreement. If the contract was prepaid, then determine whether the agreement provides for a refund for the unused portion.

Even if the contract does not provide for a refund, you may be able to get the owner of the gym to agree to assigning the remaining membership to an heir of the decedent's Estate. Such an assignment is good public relations as well as a means of generating new business should the heir decide to purchase his own membership.

SERVICE CONTRACT

Many people purchase appliance service contracts to have their appliances serviced in the event that an appliance should need repair. If the decedent had a security system then he may have had a service contract with a company to monitor the system and contact the police in the event of a break-in.

If the decedent had a service contract, then you need to locate it and determine whether it can be assigned to the new owner of the property. If the contract is assignable, the new owner can reimburse the decedent's Estate for the unused portion. If the contract cannot be assigned, then once the property is transferred, try to obtain a refund for the unused portion of the contract.

FILING THE WILL WITH THE COURT

Anyone who has possession of the decedent's original Will needs to file it with the Probate Court in the county of the decedent's residence. If the decedent owned property in Ohio, but did not live here, the Will needs to be deposited with the Probate Court in the county where the decedent's property is located (ORC 2107.11).

You can find directions to the court house on the Internet at the Web site of the National Center For State Courts.

 NATIONAL CENTER FOR STATE COURTS
http://www.ncsconline.org

The judge will accept an original Will only and not a copy, so it is important to hand carry the original document to the Court. If you are the Executor or Personal Representative named in the Will, you can give the Will to your attorney to file with the Court when he begins the Probate procedure. Make a copy of the Will for your own records before delivering it to the Court or to your attorney, but don't alter the Will by removing its staples.

If you believe that Probate is not necessary, it is still a good idea to promptly deposit the Will with the Court. The Clerk will keep it on file with the Probate Court in the event it turns out that Probate is necessary at some later date.

OUT OF STATE RESIDENT

If the decedent owned property in Ohio, but did not live here, the Will can be deposited with the Probate Court in the county where the decedent's property is located. However, read the next page before doing so.

PROBATING OUT OF STATE PROPERTY

If the decedent had his residence in Ohio and owned property in another state, you may need to conduct the initial Probate in Ohio and an *ancillary* (secondary) Probate in the other state. If the decedent had his residence in another state and owned property in Ohio, it may need to be the other way around. You may need to conduct the initial Probate in the other state (ORC 2129.05, 2129.06).

If you are going to be Personal Representative, and the decedent was a resident of another state, before depositing the Will with the Court, consult with an experienced Probate attorney in each state to determine where the initial Probate should be conducted. Convenience is important, but there are other things you need to consider:

COST OF PROBATE
Ask each attorney whether the location of the initial Probate procedure will have an effect on the total cost of Probate.

WHO INHERITS IF NO WILL
The Laws of Descent vary significantly state to state. If the decedent died without a Will, it is important to determine whether the location of the initial Probate procedure will change who, or how much each heir will inherit.

ESTATE/INHERITANCE TAXES
Determine whether the location of the initial procedure will have an impact on the amount of taxes that need to be paid.

WILL DRAFTED IN ANOTHER STATE OR COUNTRY

A Will that was drafted in another state or country can be accepted into Probate in Ohio, provided:

☑ the Will complies with the law of the state or country that was in force at the time the Will was signed - or -

☑ if the decedent was a resident of another state, the Will was prepared and signed according to the laws of that state - or -

☑ the Will was prepared and signed according to current Ohio law (ORC 2107.18). See Chapter 5 for a discussion of what constitutes a valid Will in Ohio.

A Will drafted in another country will be interpreted according to Ohio law, regardless of whether entire Probate procedure is conducted here or whether the initial Probate is the other country and an ancillary Probate conducted here (ORC 2129.07).

☎ LAWYER

WILL DRAFTED IN ANOTHER LANGUAGE

If the Will is written in a language other than English, you will need to have it translated. Consult with an attorney to determine what proof the judge will require in order to accept the translated Will into Probate as a true and correct translation of the original.

THE MISSING WILL

People tend to put off making a Will until they think they need to. For many, that need arises when they are elderly and/or seriously ill and have property that they want to leave to someone. It is uncommon for a young person to have a Will; but those who are aged, and with significant assets, usually have one. A survey conducted for the American Association of Retired Persons ("AARP") found that the probability of having a Will increases with age. Forty-four percent of those surveyed who were between the ages of 50 to 54 had a Will. This increased to 85% for those 80 and older.

Those who make a Will usually tell the person they appoint as Executor of the existence of the Will. Chances are that someone, in the decedent's circle of family and friends, knows whether there is a Will. If you believe that the decedent had a Will, but you cannot find it, there are at least three places to check out:

⇨   THE DECEDENT'S ATTORNEY
Look at the decedent's checkbook for the past few years and see whether he paid any attorney fees. If you are able to locate the decedent's attorney, then call and inquire whether the attorney ever drafted a Will for the decedent, and if so, whether the attorney has the original Will in his possession. If he has the Will, then ask him to forward it to the Probate Court in the county of the decedent's residence. Asking the attorney to forward the Will to the court does not obligate you to employ the attorney should you later find that you need the assistance of an attorney for the Probate administration.

⇨ **THE CLERK OF THE PROBATE COURT**

Ohio law gives a resident the right to deposit his Will in the office of the judge of the Probate Court in the county of his residence. At the time of deposit the Will maker will indicate who is to be given the Will once he dies. The Clerk will give the Will maker a *Certificate of Deposit* evidencing the receipt of his Will (ORC 2107.07).

If you cannot locate a Certificate of Deposit, contact the Probate Court in the county where the decedent lived and ask whether a Will was deposited with the judge. If the decedent lived in other counties in Ohio during his life-time, check with the Clerk of the Probate Court in each of those counties.

⇨ **THE SAFE DEPOSIT BOX**

Some people keep their original Will in a safe deposit box. If you believe that the decedent had a Will but you cannot find it, then check to see if the decedent had a safe deposit box. If he did, you will need to gain entry to that box to see whether the Will is in the box. See the end of this Chapter for an explanation of how to gain entry to the safe deposit box.

 **A COPY OF THE WILL AND NO ORIGINAL**

A person can revoke his Will simply by destroying it i.e., by ripping it up, or by writing over it in such a manner as to indicate that the Will is cancelled or revoked (ORC 2107.33). If you have a copy of the Will and cannot find the original, the judge will presume that the decedent revoked his Will by destroying it.

If you believe the original was not revoked but is lost, or accidentally destroyed, you can ask the Probate Court to admit a copy of the Will to Probate.

Under Ohio law, a copy of the Will can be admitted to Probate, provided it can be proven that:
☑ the document offered is a true copy of the original Will, AND
☑ the Will was signed with the formalities as required by the state where the Will was signed.

Anyone can successfully block the admission of the lost or destroyed Will to Probate, if he can prove that the Will maker revoked his Will (ORC 2107.26)

If you wish to have a lost Will admitted to Probate, you will need to employ an attorney experienced in Probate matters to present your case to the Court.

ACCESSING THE SAFE DEPOSIT BOX

If the decedent leased a safe deposit box in his name only, or jointly with another, once the lessor (bank or financial institution) learns of the death, they will restrict entry to the box. Under Ohio law, the safe deposit box may be opened in the presence of an employee of the bank. Ohio statute 5731.39 (F) requires Ohio Tax Commissioner, or his agent be present when the box is opened so that he may take an inventory of the contents of the box. Section (G) (1) of the statute gives the Tax Commissioner the right to waive inspection of the box. As of July, 2006, the Frequently Asked Question ("FAQ") section of the Department of Taxation Estate Tax Web site reports that the Commissioner is not inspecting the contents of the safe deposit box at this time.

This being the case, the decedent's safe deposit box may be opened in the presence of a bank employee, and any of the following items removed:

> ⊳ the decedent's Will
> ⊳ the deed to a burial plot
> ⊳ any insurance policy

The bank employee will make a written record of any Will, deed, or insurance policy that is removed.

If you wish to examine the contents of the box to determine if the any of those items are in it, you should call and ask what documents they require in order to allow the inspection. You also need to ask whether there will be any bank charge for opening the box to remove these items.

Most companies want a certified copy of the death certificate and identification of the person removing these items. You may need to wait until you have a copy of the death certificate before you will be allowed to inspect the contents of the box.

Other than the Will, insurance policies and deed to a burial lot, nothing may be removed from the safe deposit box without authority from the Probate Court. If there are other valuables in the box, some kind of Probate procedure will be needed in order to get possession of those items.

See Chapter 6 for an explanation of what type of Probate procedure may be necessary to get possession of the contents of the decedent's safe deposit box.

After examining the contents of the box, you can determine whether it is necessary to keep the box open during the administration of the Estate, or whether the lease can be cancelled and the balance of the rental fee refunded to the decedent's Estate.

Once you have located the decedent's property you may think the next step is to determine who gets to inherit that property. But some of that property may be needed to pay monies owed by the decedent; so the next step is to determine what, if any, bills need to be paid.

And that is the topic of the next chapter.

What Bills Need To Be Paid? 4

The Personal Representative has the duty to be sure that all valid *claims* (demands for payment) are paid. If the decedent had debts, but no money or property, then of course there is no way to pay a claim against the decedent's Estate. The only remaining question is whether anyone else is responsible to pay for the monies owed. If the decedent was married, the first person the creditor will look to is the decedent's spouse. To understand the basis of this expectation, you need to know a bit of the history of our legal system.

Our laws are derived from the English Common Law. Under early English Common Law, a single woman had the right to own property in her own name and also the right to contract to buy or sell property; but when she married, her legal identity merged with her spouse. She could not hold property free from her husband's claim or control. She could no longer enter into a contract without her husband's permission.

Once married, a woman became financially dependent on her husband. He, in turn, became legally responsible to provide his wife with basic necessities — food, clothing, shelter and medical services. If anyone provided basic necessities to his wife, then regardless of whether the husband agreed to be responsible for the debt, he became obliged to pay for them. This law was called the DOCTRINE OF NECESSARIES.

States in America departed from English Common Law by enacting a series of Married Women's Rights Acts. The Ohio legislature passed laws giving a married person (man or woman) the right to own property, and to enter into a contract the same as if single (ORC 3103.05, 3103.07).

Court cases followed that tested whether the Doctrine of Necessaries still applied. Judges had to decide:

If a wife can own property and contract to pay for her own necessities, should her husband be responsible for such debts in the event she does not have enough money to pay for them?

And if it the husband is responsible for his wife's necessities, should she be responsible for his?

In Ohio, the answer to both of these questions is "yes." Although some states abolished the law altogether, other states, including Ohio, decided to apply the Doctrine equally to both sexes, making the husband responsible to pay for his wife's necessities and the wife responsible to pay for her husband's necessities. Each partner is responsible to contribute to the support and maintenance of the family. If one of the partner is unable to support himself, the other partner is required, by Ohio law, to assist with support, as much as he is able. If the other partner (the "supporting partner") neglects to do so, anyone who provides necessities has the right to demand payment from the supporting partner — whether or not he agreed to be responsible to pay for those necessities (ORC 3103.03).

This right continues after death. If the decedent was married and owed money for necessities, the creditor can demand payment from the decedent's Estate. But if there are not sufficient funds to pay the debt, he can look to the spouse for payment.

JOINT DEBTS

A *joint debt* is a debt that two or more people are responsible to pay. Usually the contract or promissory note states that the parties agree to *joint and several liability*, meaning they all agree to pay the debt and each of them promises to be personally responsible to pay the debt. A joint debt can also be in the form of monies owed by one person with payment guaranteed by another person. If the person who owes the money does not pay, then the *guarantor* (the person who guaranteed payment) is responsible to make payment.

PAYING FOR THE JOINT DEBT

If the decedent was jointly responsible with someone else to pay for monies owed, whether or not the contract or promissory note says so, Ohio law considers the debt to be joint and several. This means that as of the date of his death, the decedent's Estate is solely liable for the entire balance of any joint debt (ORC 2117.31). Of course if there is no money in the decedent's Estate, the creditor will look to the surviving joint debtor for payment.

 **SPOUSE** ⟶ JOINT SPOUSAL DEBTS

Loans signed by the decedent and his spouse are joint debts, as are charges on credit cards that both were authorized to use. Property taxes are a joint debt if the decedent and the spouse both owned the property. All of these debts may be paid from the decedent's Estate. If there are insufficient Estate funds, the surviving spouse is liable for the entire debt.

Suppose all of the decedent's funds are held jointly with a family member (not his spouse) and the joint owner of the bank account did not agree to pay those debts? Can the creditor require that half of the joint funds be set aside to pay the debt?

The answer depends on how the account was set up. As we will see in Chapter 5, there are different ways to hold property jointly with another. If the property is owned *Jointly With Right of Survivorship*, the survivor owns the property as of the date of death. Ohio courts have ruled that the creditors of the deceased joint owner have no right to demand money from that account unless the surviving joint owner is responsible for the decedent's debt (*In re Certificates of Deposit issued by Hocking Valley Bank of Athens Co.*, 569 N.E.2d 484 (Ohio, 1991)).

NO EXEMPTION FOR TAXES

The beneficiary of the decedent's joint account has no obligation to use the joint account funds to pay the decedent's creditors; however, the decedent's share of the joint account is included as part of the decedent's *Taxable Estate*. If federal or state taxes are due, whoever takes the decedent's share of the joint account may be required to pay whatever taxes are due on the decedent's share of the account. But if the decedent gave instructions in his Will that all his taxes are to be paid from monies set aside for that purpose, the Personal Representative will follow those directions and pay the taxes.

NO MONEY — NO PROPERTY

If the decedent owed money then the debt needs to be paid from assets owned by the decedent — which leads to the next question, "Did the decedent have any money in his own name when he died?"

If the decedent died without any money or property in his name, then there is no money to pay any creditor. The only question that remains is whether anyone else is liable to pay those bills. The issue of payment most often arises in relation to services provided by nursing homes. When a person enters a nursing home, he is usually too ill to speak for himself or even sign his name. In such cases, the nursing home administrator may ask the spouse or a family member to sign a battery of papers on behalf of the patient before allowing the patient to enter the facility. Buried in that battery of papers may be a statement that the family member agrees to be responsible for payment to the nursing home. If the family member refuses to guarantee payment and the patient's finances are limited, the facility may refuse to admit the patient.

Under the Federal Nursing Home Reform Law, a nursing home that accepts Medicare or Medicaid payments is prohibited from requiring a family member to guarantee payment as a condition of allowing the patient to enter that facility (42 U.S.C. 13951-3(c)(5)(A)(ii)).

Nonetheless, it is common practice for a nursing home, in effect, to say "Either someone agrees to pay for the patient's bill or you need to find a different facility."

For those patients who are single, their position is understandable. The nursing home can require payments from the patient's spouse, but if he is single, no one is responsible to make payments should the patient's monies run out. Most nursing homes are business establishments and not charitable organizations. Even not-for-profit organizations must cover their costs. The nursing home must be paid for the services they provide or they soon will be out of business. For an insolvent patient, the solution is to have the patient admitted to the facility as a Medicaid patient.

But suppose the decedent had some money when he entered the nursing home and you agreed to guarantee payment to the nursing home. What if you feel that you were coerced into signing as a guarantor?

Are you now liable to pay the decedent's final nursing home bill if your family member died without funds?

An experienced Elder Law attorney will be able to answer these questions after examining the documents that you signed and the conditions under which the patient entered the nursing home.

PAYING THE DECEDENT'S BILLS

If the decedent was married and no Probate procedure is necessary, then the surviving spouse needs to make provision for paying bills they were both responsible to pay. If the decedent was not married and he owned property belonging to him alone, such as a bank account, securities or real property, then paying monies owed by the decedent falls to the Personal Representative.

Once he is appointed, the Personal Representative will try to locate of the decedent's creditors so that he can give them written notice of the death. A creditor who receives such notice will have 30 days to come forward and present his claim (ORC 2117.07).

The Personal Representative needs to look over each claim and decide whether that claim is valid. The problem with making that decision is that the decedent is not here to say whether he actually received the goods and services that are now being billed to his Estate.

That is especially the case for medical or nursing care bills. An example of improper billing brought to the attention of this author was that of a bill submitted for a physical examination of the decedent. The bill listed the date of the examination as July 10th, but the decedent died on July 9th. Other incorrect billings may not be as obvious, so each invoice needs to be carefully examined.

If the Personal Representative decides to challenge a bill, and is unable to settle the matter with the creditor, then the Probate court will decide whether the debt is valid and should be paid.

MEDICAL BILLS COVERED BY INSURANCE

If the decedent had health insurance you may receive an invoice stamped "THIS IS NOT A BILL." This means the health care provider has submitted the bill to the decedent's health insurance company and expects to be paid by them. If the decedent was receiving Medicare, you will receive a ***Medicare Summary Notice*** listing all of the services or supplies that were billed to Medicare for the prior 30 days. If the decedent was receiving Medicare Part B drugs, such as certain cancer drugs, you may receive two Medicare Summary Notices, one for the doctor's visit and for medication given to the decedent during the visit. The medication notice will let you know if the doctor administered drug is approved or denied.

Even though payment is not requested, it is important to verify that the bill is valid for two reasons:

➤ LATER LIABILITY

If the insurer refuses to pay the claim, the facility will seek payment from whoever is in possession of the decedent's property, and that may reduce the amount inherited by the beneficiaries.

➤ INCREASED HEALTH CARE COSTS

Regardless of whether the decedent was covered by a private health care insurer or Medicare, improper billing increases the cost of health insurance to all of us. Consumers pay high premiums for health coverage. We, as taxpayers, all share the cost of Medicare. If unnecessary or fraudulent billing is not checked, then ultimately, we all pay. If you believe that you have come across a case of Medicare fraud, you can call the ANTI-FRAUD HOTLINE (800) 447-8477 and report the incident to the Office of the Inspector General of the United States Department of Health and Human Services.

HOW TO CHECK MEDICARE BILLING

The structure of Medicare has changed giving people the option of staying with the *Original Medicare Plan* or choosing a *Medicare Advantage Plan* such as a Medicare Health Maintenance Organization ("HMO"), or other Medicare Health Plans. Coverage depends on which plan is chosen. You need to determine whether the decedent was covered under the Original Medicare Plan, or some other Medicare Plan. The publication *Medicare and You* explains coverage under the different options. See page 53 of this book, to obtain a copy of the booklet. Coverage under any of the other plans is explained in the membership materials given to the decedent at the time he signed up for the plan.

BILLING UNDER THE ORIGINAL MEDICARE PLAN

ASSIGNMENT

An important billing question for those under the Original Medicare Plan is whether the health care provider agreed to accept Medicare *assignment*, meaning that they agreed to accept the Medicare-approved amount. If so, the patient is responsible to pay any Medicare deductible and coinsurance amounts (usually 20% of the approved amount).

Doctors and health care providers who do not accept assignment, are limited in the amount they can charge for a Medicare covered service. The highest they can charge is **15%** over the Medicare-approved amount. This *Limiting Charge* applies only to certain services and does not apply to supplies and equipment. For more information about assignment you can call (800) 633-4227 for your free copy of *Does your doctor or supplier accept "assignment?"* or you can down-load the publication from the Medicare Website: http://www.medicare.gov

ADVANCE BENEFICIARY NOTICE

For those who are in the Original Medicare Plan, a doctor or a supplier may give notice saying that Medicare probably will not pay for the service that is about to be provided. This is called an ***Advance Beneficiary Notice***.

Other Medicare Plans also notify the patient in the event that the service is not covered under the plan. If the patient still wants the service after receiving such notice, he will be asked to sign an agreement stating that he will pay for the service in the event that Medicare does not pay.

If all of this appears confusing, it is.
To check the decedent's Medicare billing, you need the answers to the following questions:

What is the plan?
Determine whether the decedent was in the Original Medicare Plan or some other Medicare Health Plan.

What is covered under the plan?
The *Medicare and You* booklet explains what is covered under the Original Medicare Plan. You will need a copy of the membership materials for the Medicare Advantage Plans to determine what is covered under that plan.

Does the Provider accept Assignment?
If the decedent was in the Original Medicare Plan, you need to determine whether the health care provider accepted assignment; and if not, whether the Limiting Charge applies to the services provided. If assignment is accepted, or the Limiting Charge applies, you need to determine the Medicare-approved amount.

Did the decedent agree to pay?

Check to see whether the decedent was given notice that the service would not be covered by Medicare; and if so, whether he signed a contract agreeing to pay in the event that Medicare refuses to pay.

Did the decedent have a Medigap Policy?

A ***Medigap Policy*** is a health insurance policy sold by private insurance in accordance with state and federal law. It is Medicare Supplemental Insurance. If the decedent had a Medigap Policy, get a copy of the contract and see if the goods or services provided are covered under the Policy.

DENIAL OF MEDICARE COVERAGE

If the health care provider reports to you that a service provided to the decedent is not covered by Medicare, or if the facility submits the bill and Medicare refuses to pay, check to see if you agree with that ruling by getting answers to the questions on the prior page. You can appeal that decision if you believe that the decedent was wrongly denied coverage.

If the decedent was in the Original Medicare Plan, you will find information about how to file an appeal on the Medicare Summary Notice. If he opted for a Medicare Advantage Plan or some other Medicare Health Plan, you will find that information in his health care plan materials. The book *Your Medicare Rights and Protections* (CMS Pub. No. 10112) contains information about appeals. You can get a free copy by calling (800) 633-4227 or by down-loading it from the Medicare Website. http://www.medicare.gov.

The U.S. Department of Health and Human Services is in charge of Medicare Appeals. They hold hearings with video conference equipment or by telephone. They allow you to appeal in person before an Administrative Law Judge only if "special or extraordinary circumstances exist."

Even if an in-person hearing is allowed, a hearing before an Administrative Law Judge is currently available in only four locations Miami, Florida; Cleveland, Ohio; Irvine, California and Arlington, Virginia. Those who insist on a face-to-face hearing lose their right to receive a decision within 90 days, so it may take considerable time before the matter is settled.

GETTING HELP WITH THE APPEAL

You can appeal the decision yourself, but it is best to first call the OHIO SENIOR HEALTH INSURANCE INFORMATION PROGRAM ("OSHIIP") and learn how to proceed with your appeal. You can call OSHIIP toll free at (800) 686-1578 or visit the Consumer Services section of the OHIO DEPARTMENT OF INSURANCE Web site for information.

 OHIO DEPARTMENT OF INSURANCE
http://www.ins.ohio.gov/ConsumerServ/Oshiip

If you want an attorney to assist with your appeal, call the Ohio Bar at (800) 282-6556 for a referral to an attorney who is experienced in Medicare appeals. Some attorneys work *pro bono* (literally for the public good; i.e. without charge) but most charge a fee. Federal statute 42 U.S.C. 406(a)(2)(A) limits the amount an attorney may charge for a successful Medicare appeal to 25% of the amount recovered or $4,000, whichever is the smaller amount.

DECEDENT ON MEDICAID

Medicaid is a program that provides medical and long term nursing care for people with low income and limited resources. The program is funded jointly by the federal and state government. Federal law requires the state to recover monies spent on behalf of a Medicaid recipient who was 55 or older when he received Medicaid assistance. The state will seek reimbursement from a recipient's Estate for money spent on his behalf while he was a resident of a nursing facility, or an intermediate care facility for the mentally retarded or any Home and Community Based Waiver services (ORC 5111.11).

There usually is no money to recover because to qualify for Medicaid in Ohio, a single person may not have more than $1,500 in spendable assets. But sometimes it happens that the person on Medicaid dies and his Estate later receives money perhaps as part of a settlement of a lawsuit. Also, it could happen that he owned a home in his name only. In general, owning a home does not disqualify a person from receiving Medicaid, however if he received Medicaid benefits after age 55, the state has the right to place a lien on that home and seek recovery from the proceeds of the sale of the house once he dies. However, federal law prohibits the foreclosure of that lien until the surviving spouse, and/ or the decedent's minor or disabled child are no longer living in the home (42 U.S.C. 1396(p), ORC 5111.111). If you have a question about the right of the state to recover money from the decedent's Estate, call your local county **OFFICE OF JOB AND FAMILY SERVICES** or the **OHIO DEPARTMENT OF AGING** at (800) 266-4346.

Sometimes it happens that the decedent had money or property titled in his name only, but he also had a significant amount of debt. In such cases the beneficiaries may wonder whether they should go through a Probate procedure if there will be little, if anything, left after the creditors are paid. Before making the decision consider that some assets are protected under Ohio law. Statute 2329.66 contains a list of items that are exempt from the claims of creditors both before and after death. Included in that list are the following:

✧ THE DECEDENT'S PENSION PLAN ✧

If the decedent had a pension or retirement plan, the extent to which the proceeds are exempt from the claims of his creditors depends on the type of pension plan.

PUBLIC EMPLOYEE PENSION PLAN

If the decedent was a public employee of the state of Ohio, such as a fireman, policeman, teacher, etc. his pension plan is exempt from creditor claims, not only for the decedent's Estate but also for the beneficiary of the plan. Death benefits from the decedent's retirement fund are also exempt from the claims of his creditors (ORC 145.56, 2329.66 (A) (10)(a), 3307.41, 3309.66, 5505.22).

FEDERAL PENSION PLAN

If the decedent had a Federal retirement plan identified by the Internal Revenue Code of 1986 as 219, 402(c), 403(a)(4), 403(b)(8), 408 (d)(3), 408A(c)(3)(B), 408A(d)(3) and 530(d)(5) (this includes IRA and Roth IRA accounts), the monies in the account are exempt from the claims of creditors. All monies received by a beneficiary of such plans are protected from the decedent's creditors (ORC 2329.66 (A) (10)(c)).

PRIVATE PENSION PLAN
If the decedent had a pension plan with a private (non-governmental) company or if the decedent had a Keogh or "H.R. 10" plan, the proceeds from such plans are exempt to the decedent's dependents, but only up to the amount that is reasonably necessary for the support of those dependents (ORC 2329.66 (A) (10)(b) & (d)). If the decedent did not have any dependents, these funds are available to pay valid claims against the decedent's Estate.

NO EXEMPTION FOR TAXES
In general, income taxes are not paid when money is placed in a retirement plan. Taxes are paid when the monies are withdrawn from the account regardless of whether the monies are withdrawn by the retiree or the person he named as beneficiary of the retirement plan. If you are inheriting money from the decedent's pension, annuity or retirement allowance, you will need to pay taxes on those money (ORC 3307.41). You will need to consult with an accountant or an attorney to determine how much money needs to be set aside to pay for federal and Ohio state income taxes.

✧ GROUP INSURANCE ✧
If the decedent was covered by a group insurance policy as part of his employment, all of the proceeds of the policy, paid to a named beneficiary, are exempt from the decedent's creditors (ORC 3917.05).

✧ BENEFITS FROM A FRATERNAL BENEFIT SOCIETY ✧
Any benefit that is payable by a fraternal benefit society (e.g., AARP, American Legion, Kiwanis, Lighthouse for the Blind, Rotary Club, etc.) is free of the monies owed by the decedent. In fact, benefits paid by a fraternal benefit society are free from the claims of the creditors of the decedent member of the society AND from the creditors of the beneficiary of those funds (ORC 3921.18).

✧ LIFE INSURANCE PROCEEDS AND ANNUITIES ✧

The proceeds of the decedent's life insurance policy, or annuity are inherited free of the claims of the decedent's creditors, provided the policy is payable to any of the following people:

⇨ the decedent's spouse

⇨ the decedent's child

⇨ anyone who is dependent on his spouse or child

⇨ charitable institution as described by section 170, 501(c)(3), 2055, or 2522 of the Internal Revenue Code

⇨ any creditor named as beneficiary of the policy

If the beneficiary of the policy is not one of those mentioned above, all of the proceeds are available to pay the decedent's debts.

Regardless of the identity of the beneficiary, if the policy or annuity was purchased to defraud a creditor, the proceeds can be used to pay money owed. For example, if someone is unable to pay his debts, and yet uses whatever money he has to buy a life insurance policy, the creditor can demand that the premium paid for the policy be subtracted from the proceeds of the policy and be used to pay monies owed to him by the decedent (ORC 3911.10).

✧ WRONGFUL DEATH AWARD ✧

As discussed in Chapter 1, the Personal Representative has the right to bring a law suit on behalf of the decedent's Estate if the death was caused by the wrongful act of a person or company. Monies received by a dependent of the decedent are creditor proof, to the extent reasonably necessary for the support of that person, and any of his dependents (ORC 2329.66 (A) (12) (b)).

In general, money received under the VICTIMS OF CRIME COMPENSATION PROGRAM as described in Chapter 1, are also creditor proof (ORC 2743.66 (D)).

✧ CREDITOR PROTECTION FOR THE SPOUSE ✧

As discussed on the previous page, if the decedent named his spouse as the beneficiary of his life insurance policy, whatever the value of that policy, the spouse can take the proceeds and not be required to use any of those funds to pay monies owed by the decedent, unless, of course, the surviving spouse is jointly responsible for the debt. Other items that the spouse can inherit free of the decedent's creditor claims are the Support Allowance, the family car and boat, and her Dower Rights:

⇨ THE SUPPORT ALLOWANCE

If the decedent left a spouse and/or minor children, then they are entitled to receive up to $40,000 in money or property free of creditor claims. The property can be personal property or real property such as the decedent's home. If one or more of the minor children are not children of the surviving spouse, the Probate court will divide the $40,000 equitably between the spouse and minor children (ORC 2106.13).

⇨ RESIDENCY PROTECTION

If a health care provider (hospital, doctor, etc.) has a judgment for monies owed for providing health care to the decedent, that judgment becomes a lien on the decedent's home. If the residence is transferred to the surviving spouse or minor child of the decedent, the health care provider cannot force the sale of the residence to pay for the judgment. Payment is postponed until the home is sold or transferred to someone other than the surviving spouse or minor child (ORC 2329.66 (A)(1)(a)).

⇨   THE FAMILY CAR AND BOAT

If the decedent owned automobiles in his name only, his spouse has the right to two of the cars provided the value of the cars is not greater than $40,000. If the spouse takes two cars, the Probate court may have the cars appraised and may reduce the Support Allowance by the lesser value of the two cars. This also applies to the decedent's motorcycle, and truck if the truck was used for transportation for the decedent or his family.

If the decedent named someone (not his spouse) in his Will, to inherit his motor vehicle, it is not available for the spouse to take. Similarly, if the decedent owned one watercraft and/or an outboard motor and he did not make a gift of these items in his Will, the spouse is entitled to keep these items (ORC 2106.13, ORC 2106.18, 2106.19).

If the decedent had a loan on his car or boat, whoever inherits these items becomes responsible to pay the balance of that loan — else the creditor can repossess the car or boat. Other than loans on the car or boat, the spouse has the right to take these items free from the decedent's creditors. The motor vehicles, watercraft and outboard motor are not considered to be assets of the decedent's Estate.

⇨   DOWER RIGHTS IN REAL PROPERTY

Dower rights are another relic of English law retained by the state of Ohio. As with the Doctrine of Necessaries, the law is related to early English law that banned a married woman from owning property in her own name. To assure that a married woman was not left destitute once her husband died, English law gave the wife the right to occupy and receive rents from one-third of all of her husband's property. This right was limited to her life-time, so it was called a *Life Estate*. Once she died, the property went back to her deceased husband's Estate to be inherited by his heirs or next of kin.

As with the Doctrine of Necessaries, each state developed its own set of laws relating to the right of a widow (and widower) to inherit property. In Ohio, both husband and wife have a Dower right to a Life Estate in one-third of all of the real property owned by his spouse during the marriage. However once a partner dies, the surviving spouse no longer is entitled to a Life Estate in that property. The Dower share is replaced by an *Elective Share* of the decedent's Estate. The Elective Share is the amount the spouse inherits under Ohio's Laws of Descent and Distribution. Those Laws are explained in the next chapter.

Neither partner has the right to mortgage, sell or in any way transfer real property without written permission from his spouse because that diminishes the spouse's Elective Share. If the decedent transferred or mortgaged property during the marriage without getting permission from his spouse, the spouse can assert his Dower rights in that property; and that right has priority over the creditors of the decedent (ORC 2103.02).

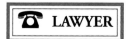 **DOWER PROPERTY TRANSFERRED WITHOUT PERMISSION**

If the decedent transferred or mortgaged real property during his marriage without getting permission from his spouse, the spouse may have Dower rights in that property and should consult with an attorney to determine his rights in that property.

DOWER RIGHTS MAY BE RELINQUISHED
A spouse who leaves to live with another in adultery, forfeits his Dower rights unless his spouse pardons and forgives him (ORC 2103.05).

✧ THERE IS A PRIORITY OF PAYMENT ✧

The next thing to consider is that not all probate debts are equal. Ohio statute (ORC 2117.25) establishes an order of priority for payment of claims made against the decedent's estate:

CLASS 1:   COST OF ADMINISTRATION
Top priority goes to the cost of the probate procedure including attorney's fees and fees charged by the Personal Representative.

CLASS 2:   FUNERAL EXPENSES
Second in priority is the decedent's funeral, burial and grave marker expenses but only up to $2,000. The next $1,000 of the bill becomes a Class 6 debt; and the remaining monies owed becomes a Class 9 debt.

CLASS 3:   THE SUPPORT ALLOWANCE
Any of the property set aside as the Support Allowance is protected from the decedent's creditors. The only items that must be paid before the Support Allowance can be distributed are the costs associated with the Probate and the Class 2 funeral expenses.

CLASS 4:   FEDERAL CLAIMS
Fourth in line for payment is money owed to the federal government, such as back income taxes or penalties.

CLASS 5:   EXPENSES OF THE LAST ILLNESS
Unpaid medical or nursing care costs are 5th in priority of payment.

CLASS 6:   NEXT $1,000 OF FUNERAL EXPENSE

If the total bill of the funeral director exceeds $2,000, then the next $1,000 of that bill is a Class 6 debt.

CLASS 7:   MONIES DUE TO THE STATE OF OHIO

Monies owed by the decedent to the state of Ohio are seventh in priority. This includes back income taxes (including interest and penalties), and money owed to the state for reimbursement of medical assistance given to the decedent after the age of 55 (ORC 2117.18).

CLASS 8:   WAGES TO DECEDENT'S EMPLOYEE

If the decedent owed anyone money for manual labor performed for the decedent within 12 months of his death, then up to $300 per person is a Class 8 debt. If the decedent owed an employee more than $300, the balance due becomes a Class 9 debt.

CLASS 9:   ALL OTHER DEBTS

Ohio law requires that claims against the Probate Estate be paid in the above order. For example, suppose the decedent left enough money to pay for the Probate procedure, funeral expenses and for the Support Allowance with $30,000 left over. If there are no other valid claims against the Estate debts, the beneficiaries get the $30,000.

Suppose instead that he left a hospital bill of $30,000 and a doctor's bill of $10,000 (both Class 5 debts). The $20,000 will be prorated with the hospital getting $15,000 and the doctor getting $5,000. There will be nothing left to pay any other claim. There will be nothing left for anyone to inherit (ORC 2117.25).

✦ THERE IS A STATUTE OF LIMITATIONS ✦

There are federal and state laws that set time periods for pursuing a claim. Anyone who wishes to take court action must do so within the time set by the given Statute of Limitation. For example, a law suit for the wrongful death of the decedent must be filed within two years of the death (ORC 2125.02).

There is a Statute of Limitations for a creditor to come forward and make a claim against the decedent's Estate for monies owed. Creditors have six months from the date of death to present their claims to the Personal Representative (ORC 2117.06). This period can be shortened if the Personal Representative sends the creditor written notice to present his claim within thirty days from the day the creditor receives the notice (ORC 2117.07).

There are exceptions to the six month limit such as federal and state claims, and certain liens on the decedent's property (ORC 2117.10). For example, the state of Ohio has up to one year from the decedent's date of date to file a claim for Medical Assistance provided to the decedent (ORC 2117.061).

But what if no one starts a Probate procedure? If no one begins a Probate procedure within one year from the date of death, the beneficiaries may be able to obtain possession of the decedent's assets free from creditor claims.

But read on before you decide to wait out the year.

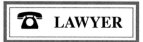

DECEDENT LEAVING CONSIDERABLE DEBT

If the decedent died leaving much debt and no property, the solution is simple. No Probate, no one gets paid. But if the decedent had property and died owing more money than the property was worth, his heirs may decide that going through Probate is not worth the effort, or they may decide to simply wait out the Statute of Limitation period and begin Probate at that time.

This may not be the best decision. Some creditors are tenacious and will use whatever legal strategy is available in order to be paid, including initiating the Probate procedure themselves. For example, if no one starts a Probate procedure, a creditor can petition (ask) the Court to be appointed as Personal Representative of the Estate (ORC 2113.06).

As we will see in Chapter 6 , a Personal Representative has much authority when conducting the Probate procedure. Family members may object to having a creditor as a Personal Representative, so there could be a court battle over who has priority to be appointed as Personal Representative.

Court battles are expensive, emotionally as well as financially. Before you decide to distance yourself from the Probate procedure, consult with an attorney experienced in Probate matters for an opinion about the best way to administer the Estate.

MONIES OWED TO THE DECEDENT

Suppose you owed money to the decedent. Do you need to pay that debt now that he is dead? That depends on whether there is some written document that says the debt is forgiven once the decedent dies. For example, suppose the decedent loaned you money to buy your home. If he left a Will saying that once he dies, your debt is forgiven, then you do not need to make any more payments. If you signed a promissory note and mortgage at the time you borrowed the money from the decedent, the Personal Representative should sign the original promissory note **PAID IN FULL** and return the note to you. If the mortgage was recorded, the Personal Representative needs to have a Satisfaction of Mortgage recorded in the county where the property is located. You should receive the recorded Satisfaction for your records.

If you owed the decedent money and there is no Will, or if there is a Will, and no mention of forgiving the debt, then you still owe the money. Money borrowed from the decedent and his spouse needs to be repaid to the spouse. Money borrowed from the decedent only, becomes an asset of the Estate of the decedent, meaning that you owe the money to the decedent's Estate. If you are one of the beneficiaries of the Estate, you may be able to deduct the money from your inheritance.

For example, suppose your father left $80,000 to be divided equally between you and your brother. If you owed your father $20,000, your father's Estate is really worth $100,000, with each child entitled to $50,000. Instead of paying the $20,000, you can agree to receive $30,000 and have the $20,000 debt forgiven. Your brother will receive the remaining $50,000.

Who Are The Beneficiaries? 5

A question that comes up early on is who is entitled to the property of the decedent. To answer the question you first need to know how the property was *titled* (owned) as of the date of death.

There are three ways to own property. The decedent could have owned property jointly with another person, or in trust for another person; or the decedent could have owned property that was titled in his name only.

In general, upon the decedent's death:

Joint Property With Right of Survivorship
belongs to the surviving joint owner.

Trust Property belongs to the beneficiary
of the Trust.

Property owned by the **decedent only**, with no provision for a non-Probate transfer to a beneficiary after death, becomes part of the decedent's Probate Estate to be distributed as part of a Probate procedure.

NOTE ⇨ If the decedent was married, his
spouse may have rights in his property.

This chapter describes each type of ownership in detail.

PROPERTY OWNED JOINTLY

Bank accounts, securities, motor vehicles, real property can all be owned jointly by two or more people. If one of the joint owners dies, the survivor(s) continue to own their share of the property. Who owns the share belonging to the decedent depends on how the joint ownership was set up.

THE JOINT BANK ACCOUNT

When a bank account is opened the depositor signs an agreement with the bank that states the terms and conditions of the account (ORC 1109.05). If the account is opened in two or more names, each depositor is given a statement of the terms and conditions of the account. The statement will say whether each depositor has authority to make a withdrawal, or whether two signatures are necessary.

If the agreement says that the owners of a joint account have a right of survivorship, should an owner of the account die, the surviving owner is free to withdraw the money from the account without the need to go through Probate, but understanding that if the account is greater than $25,000, the bank may withhold up to 25% of the account unless he gets tax clearance purposes (ORC 5731.39). See page 40.

If a joint bank account with right of survivorship is held in three names, should one of the owners die, either of the remaining owners can withdraw funds from the account. It could become a race to the bank to take the money. But that would only serve to cause hard feelings. With such an arrangement, the remaining owners need to cooperate with each other to pay any tax that is due and then divide whatever remains equitably.

JOINTLY HELD SECURITIES

You can determine whether the decedent owns a security alone or jointly with another by examining the face of the stock or bond certificate. If two names are printed on the certificate followed by a statement that the owners are "Joint Tenants With Right of Survivorship ("JTWRS")," the surviving owner can either cash in the security or ask the company to issue a new certificate in the name of the surviving owner (ORC 1701.24 (D)). As explained in Chapter 2, you will need tax clearance before making the transfer.

Each state has its own securities regulations. If a security held in two or more names, was registered or purchased in another state, and it does not indicate whether there is a right of survivorship, you need to contact the company to determine how the account was set up; i.e. with or without a right of survivorship.

If the decedent held his securities in a brokerage account, check the monthly or quarterly brokerage statement to see if the account was owned jointly. Not all brokerage firms print the name of a joint owner on the brokerage statement, so you need to contact the brokerage firm and request a copy of the contract that is the basis of the account. It may be that the account is held jointly, or perhaps the decedent named a beneficiary who now owns the account. The contract will show when the account was opened and the terms of the brokerage account. If you determine that the account is held jointly or for the benefit of someone, have the brokerage firm forward the necessary forms to transfer the securities to the proper owner or beneficiary.

JOINTLY OWNED MOTOR VEHICLE

If the decedent owned a motor vehicle *jointly with right of survivorship*, the surviving owner now owns the car 100%. In Ohio, a car may have a TRANSFER-ON-DEATH ("TOD") designation. The owner may name one or more beneficiaries of the car. If the decedent's car had a TOD designation, the beneficiary now owns the car (ORC 4505.06).

If you are the surviving joint owner, or TOD beneficiary of the car, you should have the Clerk of the Court of Common Pleas issue a new title in your own name as soon as is practicable. You might be able to get a reduced insurance rate if there is only one person insured under the policy. Also, should the surviving owner be involved in an accident, and title has officially been changed, there will not be any question regarding whether the Estate of the decedent is liable for the accident.

MOTOR VEHICLE IN DECEDENT'S NAME ONLY

As explained on Page 110, if a car, truck or motorcycle is in the decedent's name only, and he did not made provision for the transfer of the vehicle, then the surviving spouse has rights in his motor vehicle.

If the decedent was single and owned the car in his name only it goes to the beneficiaries named in the Will. If the decedent died without a Will, the car is inherited by his next of kin in the order given in the Ohio Laws of Descent and Distribution. These Laws are explained later in this Chapter. See Chapter 6 for an explanation of how to transfer title to the motor vehicle.

The name of the owner of real property is printed on the face of the deed. To determine whether the decedent owned the property jointly with another person, you need to look at the last recorded deed. (See Chapter 3 if you cannot locate the deed.) The deed may be called a "SURVIVORSHIP DEED" as in the following example

SURVIVORSHIP DEED

ANN TRAYNOR, a single woman of Clark County, Ohio
for valuable consideration paid, grants to,
ALFRED CODY, a married man, of Clark County, Ohio
and FRANK RUPERT of Clark County, Ohio,
**FOR THEIR JOINT LIVES, REMAINDER
TO THE SURVIVOR OF THEM,**
whose tax-mailing address is . . .
the following described real property

. . .

Ann Traynor is the **Grantor** of the deed. That means she transferred the property to Alfred and Frank who are the **Grantees** of the deed. The Grantees have a *Survivorship Tenancy,* meaning that they are *Joint Tenants With Right of Survivorship.* Should one of the *survivorship tenants* die, the other will own the property 100% (ORC 5302.17).

Nothing need be done to establish the ownership of the survivor, however the decedent's name remains on the deed. Chapter 6 explains how to record documents that will notify anyone who is examining title to the property that the survivor is the sole owner of the property.

🗐 DEED HELD AS TENANT IN COMMON

If a deed identifies the decedent and another as **TENANTS IN COMMON**, the decedent's share of the property belongs to whomever the decedent named as his beneficiary in his Will. If the decedent died without a Will, the Ohio Laws of Descent and Distribution determine who inherits the decedent's share of the property. A Probate procedure will be necessary to transfer the decedent's share of the property to the proper beneficiary.

In Ohio, there is no implied right of survivorship. A deed must contain specific survivorship language, otherwise the Grantees own the property as Tenants In Common. For example, if a deed identifies two people as Grantees without any mention of survivorship, or if the deed identifies the Grantees as "Joint Tenants," then in each of these cases they own the property as Tenants in Common with each having an *Interest In Common* (ORC 5302.19).

 **LAWYER**   THE AMBIGUOUS DEED

Most deeds clearly state whether a surviving owner inherits the decedents share. But some deeds are not all that descriptive. For example, suppose a deed is granted to "Jay Simms OR Dale Belham, as joint tenants"

The use of the word "OR" in itself does not create a Survivorship Tenancy, nor would it make any difference if the word "AND" was used (ORC 5302.20).

Best to consult with an attorney if you have any question about how to interpret a deed.

🗎 DEED HELD AS HUSBAND AND WIFE

If a deed is dated before **APRIL 4, 1985,** and the Grantee on the deed is identified as a married couple, such as:

TODD AMES AND SUSAN AMES, HUSBAND AND WIFE

or

TODD AMES AND SUSAN AMES, TENANTS BY ENTIRETY

when one spouse dies, and providing they are married at the time of death, the surviving spouse owns the property 100%. As with a Survivorship Tenancy, documents need to be recorded so that anyone who is examining title to the property will know that the surviving spouse is now the sole owner of the property. The next Chapter explains what documents need to be recorded.

For deeds drafted on or after April 4, 1985, there is no right of survivorship for the husband or wife unless the deed is a Survivorship Deed drafted in the manner described earlier (ORC 5302.17, 5302.21).

 LAWYER   DIVORCED PRIOR TO DEATH

Generally, the final judgment or decree states who is to own real property owned by the couple after the divorce. If one of the parties died before title to their joint property was transferred to the proper owner, you need to consult with an attorney to determine who now owns the property.

▤ THE TRANSFER ON DEATH DEED

The TRANSFER ON DEATH DEED is a relatively new form of deed. It enables real property to be transferred to a beneficiary without going through Probate, with the added advantage of giving the owner of the property complete control of the property during his lifetime. For example, a mother can sign a Transfer On Death Deed giving the property to her children once she is deceased:

TRANSFER ON DEATH DEED

AMANDA SMITH, a single woman, of Hamilton County, Ohio, for valuable consideration paid, if any, grants to Henry Smith whose tax mailing address is 123 Main Street, Cincinnati, Ohio and to Richard Smith whose tax mailing address is 4 State Street. Columbus, Ohio
TRANSFER ON DEATH TO
HENRY SMITH AND RICHARD SMITH, BENEFICIARIES
the following described real property

. . .

The Grantees (Henry and Richard) have no right to the property while their mother is alive. She can sell the property, or revoke this deed, without asking their permission or even notifying them that she is doing so (ORC 5302.23). If Amanda makes no change to the deed, once she dies, Henry and Richard will own the property as Tenants In Common — without the need to go through any Probate procedure.

Although they do not need to go through Probate, the sons need to have their mother's death certificate made part of the public record (ORC 5302.22 (C)). See Chapter 6 for a discussion of the transfer real property.

📄 DEED WITH A LIFE ESTATE

A *Life Estate* interest in real property means that the person who owns the Life Estate has the right to live in that property until he dies. You can identify a Life Estate interest by examining the face of the deed. If somewhere on the face of the deed you see the phrase RESERVING A LIFE ESTATE to the deceased Grantor, then the Grantee now owns the property. For example, suppose the granting paragraph of the deed reads:

> LEONA SPAULDING, a single woman
> of Clermont County
> for consideration paid, grants to,
> FRANKLIN SPAULDING of Clermont County
> for valuable consideration paid, if any,
>
> . . .
>
> the following described real property
>
> . . .
>
> RESERVING A LIFE ESTATE TO THE GRANTOR

Leona is the owner of the Life Estate. Franklin owns the *Remainder Interest* in the property. Franklin has no right to occupy the property during Leona's lifetime, but once she dies, he will own the property 100%. He will be free to take possession of the property, transfer it, or sell it, as he sees fit.

As with a survivorship tenancy, nothing need be done to establish Franklin's ownership of the property once Rose dies. However, see Chapter 6 for a discussion of documents that should be recorded to show anyone who is examining title to the property that he now owns the property.

OUT OF STATE DEEDS

The laws of the state or country where the property is located determine who inherits that property. Regardless of whether the decedent was a resident of Ohio, the laws of the state where the property is located determines who inherits that property. The laws of each state are similar, but not the same. Laws differ in how the deed needs to be worded in order to have a right of survivorship. Some states do not require the deed to specifically say there is a right of survivorship. In such states, property owned by another and the decedent as Joint Tenants may mean that there is a right of survivorship. Other states, like Ohio, require the deed to actually state that there is a right of survivorship. If not, the property is owned as a Tenancy In Common.

The rights of married couples vary significantly state to state. If the decedent was married, and owned property in his name only, his surviving spouse may have rights in that property. That is the case in the Community Property states of Arizona, California, Idaho, Louisiana, Nevada, New Mexico, Texas, Washington and Wisconsin. In other states, a surviving spouse may have Dower or other statutory rights. If the decedent owned property in another state, it is important to consult with an attorney in that state to determine who now owns the property.

 THERE COULD BE A LATER DEED

The discussion in this chapter of the different types of ownership of real property assumes that you are in possession of the most recent, valid deed. The decedent could have signed another, later deed. Before you come to a conclusion about who inherits the property it is advisable to have a title search by an attorney or a title insurance company to determine the owner of the property as of the decedent's date of death.

PROPERTY HELD IN TRUST

BANK/ SECURITY ACCOUNTS

A bank account or security account that is registered in the name of the decedent "in trust for" or "for the benefit of" someone will be turned over to the beneficiary once the financial institution has a certified copy of the death certificate (ORC 1109.06, 1151.191). If the beneficiary is a minor, the company will seek Court approval before making the transfer. If the amount is $10,000 or less, the Court may allow the funds to be transferred to whoever is caring for the child — or even to the child, himself. But more likely, he will have the funds deposited into a Trust account payable to the child when he is 18 (ORC 2111.05). See Chapter 7 for a discussion of gifts made to minors.

BANK ACCOUNT HELD BY A TRUSTEE

If the bank or security account is registered in the name of the decedent "as Trustee under a Trust Agreement," that means the decedent was the Trustee of a Trust and the bank will turn over that account to the Successor Trustee of the Trust. Banks usually require a copy of the Trust Agreement or a Certificate that identifies the Successor Trustee, so the bank should be aware of the identity of the Successor Trustee. If the Trust was amended to name a different Successor Trustee, you need to present the bank with a copy of that amendment together with a certified copy of the death certificate.

MOTOR VEHICLE

A motor vehicle held in the name of the decedent "as Trustee," continues to be Trust property. The Successor Trustee will need to contact the Bureau of Motor Vehicles to have the registration changed to that of the Successor Trustee. The Successor Trustee will then dispose of the car according to the terms of the Trust Agreement.

REAL PROPERTY

If the decedent had a Trust and put real property that he owned into the Trust, then the deed may read something like this:

> JOHN ZAMORA and MARIA ZAMORA, his wife,
> of Cuyahoga County, Ohio
> for consideration paid, grants to
> JOHN ZAMORA, **Trustee,**
> **or his successors in Trust, under the**
> **JOHN ZAMORA REVOCABLE TRUST AGREEMENT**
> DATED AUGUST 2, 2006
> the following described real property
>
> . . .

The death of the Trustee of a Trust does not change the ownership of the property. It remains in the Trust. The Trust Agreement might say whether the person who takes John's place as Trustee (the Successor Trustee) should sell or keep the property or perhaps give it to a beneficiary (ORC 5301.03). The Trust may give the Successor Trustee the right to decide what to do with the property. If you are a beneficiary of the Trust and are concerned about what the Successor Trustee will do with the property, you may want to consult with your attorney to learn about your rights under that Trust.

THE DEED OF TRUST

A Deed of Trust is very different from the above described deed. The Deed of Trust is essentially a mortgage. The owner of the property places title to the property with a Trustee as security for payment of monies owed to the lender. If the debt is not paid, then the Trustee (after proper foreclosure on the property) will deliver title to the property to the Beneficiary of the Deed of Trust, namely the lender.

PROPERTY IN DECEDENT'S NAME ONLY

If the decedent owned property that was in his name only (not jointly or in trust for someone), some sort of Probate procedure may be necessary in order to transfer the property to the proper beneficiary. Who is entitled to the decedent's Probate Estate depends on whether the decedent died with or without a Will. If he died with a valid Will, the beneficiaries of the decedent's property are identified in the Will.

If the decedent died without a valid Will, Ohio Laws of Descent determine who inherits the decedent's Probate Estate and what percentage of the Estate each heir is to receive once all the bills and costs of administering the Probate procedure are paid.

The law recognizes the right of the family to inherit the decedent's property. The law covers all possible relationships beginning with the decedent's spouse. But before we discuss the rights of the surviving spouse we need to consider whether decedent had a marriage that is considered to be valid within state of Ohio.

BEING MARRIED IN OHIO

To be married in Ohio means that a man who is at least 18, and a woman who is at least 16, have obtained a license to marry from Clerk of the Probate Court, and then, within 60 days, solemnized the marriage by a state or religious ceremony. A woman who is under 18 must first obtain parental consent or the consent of her legal custodian (ORC 3101.01, 3101.05, 3101.07).

The Clerk will not issue a marriage licence if either party is drunk or under the influence of a controlled substance. The law also prohibits a license to be issued if one of the parties has syphilis that is in a contagious stage (ORC 3101.06).

Certain unions are specifically banned with the state. Ohio law specifically prohibits the marriage of people:

- ☒ those related closer than second cousin.
- ☒ those who are currently married to another person (ORC 3101.01).

THE COMMON LAW MARRIAGE

A Common Law marriage is one that has not been solemnized by ceremony. It is more than just living together. The couple must agree to live together as man and wife, and then publicly hold themselves out as being married; i.e., tell friends, family and business acquaintances that they are married. Many states do not recognize a Common Law marriage as being valid, and have passed laws to that effect. Prior to October 10, 1991 a Common Law marriage was recognized in Ohio, however after that date a marriage entered into within Ohio, or anywhere else, is not valid unless the couple obtained a marriage license and had their union solemnized by a state or religious ceremony (ORC 3105.01, 3105.12).

If the decedent entered into a Common Law marriage within the state of Ohio, before October 10, 1991, the marriage will be recognized by the Probate Court.

Generally, the surviving spouse does not need to prove that (s)he was married to the decedent. However, if anyone raises the issue, there will need to be a Court hearing on the matter.

It is important to consult with an attorney if you have any question about the validity of the decedent's marriage.

NO SAME SEX MARRIAGES

In 1998, the federal government passed the Defense of Marriage Act, saying that for purposes of federal law, marriage is a legal union between one man and one woman (28 U.S.C. 1738C). However, for purposes of state law, whether you can marry, who you can marry, and how you can marry, are determined by the laws of the state in which you live. There is much variation state to state. Vermont and Connecticut have approved same-sex *Civil Unions.* Massachusetts allows gay marriages.

The Defense of Marriage Act also provides that no state is required to recognize the laws of another state as relating to same sex marriage. And this is the case in Ohio. Ohio law bans same sex marriages and will not recognize a marriage between those of the same gender regardless of whether that relationship is legal anywhere else (ORC 3101.01).

Some states, such as California, ban same sex marriages, yet *Domestic Partners* who are registered with the state have all of the legal rights and responsibilities allowed to a married couple in California. Ohio statute prohibits the legal extension of marital benefits to a non-marital relationship within the state of Ohio (ORC 3101.01(C)). However, a couple, of the same or different gender, still have the right to make their own private agreement. Such agreement is legally enforceable in Ohio, provided, the things to which they are agreeing is not against Ohio law.

If the decedent died **intestate** (without a Will), the state of Ohio provides one for him in the form of its *Laws of Descent and Distribution*. Those laws are also referred to as the *Laws of Intestate Succession*. Once his debts, funeral expenses, and the cost of the Probate is paid, whatever is left (his *net Probate Estate*) is distributed as follows:

✧ DECEDENT, NO SPOUSE

If the decedent was single and left descendants (child, grandchild, great-grandchild, etc.), his net Probate Estate is inherited by his descendants. If he had two or more children, all who survive him, each child is entitled to an equal share of his Estate.

If a child of the decedent died before the decedent, the share intended for that child goes to the descendants of the deceased child in equal shares (ORC 2105.06). For example, suppose the decedent was single when he died, with four children, Ann, Barry, Carl, David. If he died without a Will, each child gets 25% of his net Probate Estate (ORC 2105.11).

CHILD WITHOUT DESCENDANTS DIES BEFORE DECEDENT

If Ann dies before her father, leaving no descendants, Barry, Carl and David divide the Estate between themselves. Each inherits one-third of the net Probate Estate (ORC 2105.12).

CHILD WITH DESCENDANTS DIES BEFORE DECEDENT

Suppose instead that only Carl and David survived their father. If Ann died leaving no children and Barry died leaving 2 children, the Estate is divided into 3 shares — one for each surviving child (Carl and David) and one share for Barry's children, who split the share equally (ORC 2105.13).

This method of distributing the decedent's property when a member of a group dies before the decedent is called a *"per stirpes"* distribution.

✧ MARRIED
The share inherited by the surviving spouse depends on whether the decedent is survived by descendants:

NO DESCENDANTS, OR ALL THOSE OF SPOUSE
If the decedent left a surviving spouse and no descendants, or all of his descendants are also those of his spouse, the spouse inherits the entire net Probate Estate.

ONE DESCENDANT NOT OF HIS SPOUSE
If the decedent is survived by one child (or descendants of his child) and his spouse is not the natural or adoptive parent of that child, the spouse inherits the first $20,000, plus half of what ever remains. The other half is inherited by the child, or if the child died before the decedent, to the child's descendants, in equal shares, per stirpes.

If the decedent had more than one child, none of whom are those of the spouse, the spouse inherits the first $20,000 and one third of the remainder. That increases to $60,000 and one third of the remainder if the spouse is the natural or adopted parent of at least one of the children. The decedent's children inherit the remaining two-thirds in equal shares, per stirpes (ORC 2105.06).

✧ SINGLE, NO DESCENDANTS
If the decedent had no surviving spouse or descendant, his net Probate Estate is divided equally between his parents. If only one of his parents is alive, then all of the property goes to that parent. If neither parent is alive, his Estate is inherited by the decedent's brothers and sisters in equal shares, per stirpes. There is no distinction between a sibling of the whole or half blood. They each inherit an equal share.

If the decedent had no brothers, sisters, nephews or nieces, the Probate Estate is divided with half going to his maternal grandparents (or to the survivor of them) and the other half to his paternal grandparents (or the survivor of them). If neither maternal grandparent survived the decedent, their half goes to their descendants in equal shares, per stirpes; i.e., to the aunts and uncles or to the descendants of a deceased aunt or uncle (i.e., his cousins).

The other half goes to the next of kin on the decedent's father's side in the same manner. If there are next of kin on one side of the family only, the entire Probate Estate is inherited by the next of kin on that side of the family

We could give an example of how the Estate is distributed if the decedent is survived only by descendants of his grandparents, but we thought you might enjoy a puzzle instead:

Winston died intestate leaving $100,000. His only relatives are his mother's sister, Aunt Susie, and her children, Ramona and Abigail and a first cousin Elvis, on his father's side. How much does each relative receive?

You can check your answer by visiting the puzzle section of the Eagle Publishing Company Website:
http://www.eaglepublishing.com

NO NEXT OF KIN, BUT A STEPCHILD
If a person dies without a Will and he has absolutely no surviving next of kin, but he has stepchildren, they inherit the net Probate Estate in equal shares, per stirpes (ORC 2105.06).

THE STATE: HEIR OF LAST RESORT

If a person dies without a Will and he has absolutely no next of kin and no stepchildren, or their descendants, as a last resort, his property goes to the state of Ohio. The decedent's personal property (cash, stocks, bonds, cars, etc.) is given to the County Treasurer. The County Treasurer will use the funds for the county school system (ORC 2105.07).

 IT ISN'T ALL THAT SIMPLE

The explanation in this book of the Ohio Laws of Descent is abridged. There is much more to the law. For example, anyone who inherits property according to Ohio's Law of Descent and Distribution must survive the decedent by at least 120 hours (5 days); and if not, that share is distributed as if that person died before the decedent. This rule is not applied if to do so will result in the state of Ohio inheriting the property (ORC 2105.32).

Unless the descent is straight forward, with the decedent leaving a surviving spouse and/or children (all who survive him), it is best to consult with an attorney before you decide who is entitled to inherit the decedent's net Probate Estate.

| **Special Situation** | NO SHARE FOR KILLER |

If a beneficiary has been convicted of causing the death of the decedent, then Ohio law prohibits the killer from profiting from the crime. Property that the killer would have inherited as a beneficiary of the decedent's Will or according to the Laws of Descent and Distribution, is distributed as if the killer died before the decedent. If the killer is a beneficiary of a life insurance policy, the alternate beneficiary will get the insurance proceeds.

If the killer is found guilty by reason of insanity, then he, or his guardian, can ask the Probate court to hold a trial to determine whether the killer should have the right to inherit the decedent's property. The request must be made no later than sixty days after the killer is found guilty by reason of insanity or is found to be incompetent to stand trial for the murder (ORC 2105.19).

 **LAWYER** | LAW SUIT FOR WRONGFUL DEATH

If anyone caused an injury to the decedent that was related to his death, regardless of whether that person is convicted of a crime, the Personal Representative may sue that person for a wrongful death on behalf of the beneficiaries of the decedent's Estate. See Chapter 1 for a discussion of a wrongful death.

WHO DIED FIRST?

Sometimes it happens that two family members die simultaneously and no one knows who died first. How is the Estate of each of them distributed in such case? For example, suppose a husband and wife are killed in a car accident. How is their property distributed? As explained, to inherit under the Laws of Descent and Distribution, the beneficiary must survive the decedent by at least five days (ORC 2105.32). If neither of them had a Will, property belonging to the wife is inherited as if her husband died first, and property belonging to the husband is distributed as if the wife died first. But suppose they had property that is transferred without the need for Probate. In such case, Ohio statute provides for an orderly distribution of their respective Estates.

PROCEEDS OF A LIFE INSURANCE POLICY

Suppose the husband is insured, with his wife as the beneficiary of his life insurance policy. The proceeds of the policy will be distributed as if the wife died before her husband. The proceeds will be given to the alternate beneficiary named in the policy (ORC 2105.33)

CO-OWNERS WITH RIGHT OF SURVIVORSHIP

Property the couple owned as a Survivorship Tenancy, with no provision for who is to inherit the property should they die simultaneously, becomes a Tenancy In Common with the husband's share of the property going to his Estate and the wife's share to her Estate (ORC 2105.34).

These rules also apply to property inherited by Will or Trust unless the Will or Trust makes some different provision (ORC 2105.36).

THE RIGHTS OF A CHILD

✧ THE AFTERBORN CHILD

In Ohio, a child who was conceived prior to the decedent's death, and born to the surviving spouse after the death, has the same right to inherit as any other natural child of the decedent (ORC 2105.14).

✧ THE NON-MARITAL CHILD

A child born out of wedlock has the same rights to inherit from his mother as does one born in wedlock (ORC 2105.17). The child may inherit from his natural father provided any of the following are true:

☑ The man and the child's mother are, or have been married, and the child is born during the marriage, or within 300 days after the marriage is terminated by death, divorce or annulment, or after they separated according to a separation agreement. The man is considered to be the child's natural father, even though the marriage is later found to be invalid (ORC 3111.03).

☑ The man, his adult child, and the natural mother of the adult child file a declaration stating that the man is the child's father, and the Court issues an order declaring the man to be the child's father (ORC 2105.25).

☑ A Court determined that he was the father.

If the decedent denied he was the child's father, it will take a Court procedure to establish (or disprove) paternity.

✧ THE CHILD OF AN ASSISTED CONCEPTION

Medical technology has made important contributions to solving the problem of infertility. There are all sorts of solutions, from hormone replacement therapy, to sperm banks that provide donations anonymously, to frozen sperm and/or ova to be thawed and used at a later date, to women who serve as a Surrogate or gestation mother. Solving a set of medical problems has opened the door to a new set of legal problems. Used to be, the only question was "Who's the father?" Now it could well be "Who's the mother?"

A child born to parents using any form of assisted conception has the same rights as a child conceived the old fashioned way. If a married couple wish to use artificial insemination to conceive a child, they must do it under the supervision of a licensed physician. Both parents must sign a consent form as required by statute (ORC 3111.92, 3111.93). The consent form includes the medical history of the donor, his physical characteristics, religious and educational background.

The physician will keep the consent form confidential. It may be inspected only upon Court order (ORC 3111.92, 3111.94).

Once the child is born, the birth certificate is issued to the couple identifying them as the child's parents. The husband is treated in law as if he were the natural father of the child. If a single woman is artificially inseminated, the donor is not considered to be the child's father. He has no parental rights or responsibilities (ORC 3111.95).

✧ THE ADOPTED CHILD

An adopted child has the same right to inherit property under Ohio's Laws of Descent from his adoptive parents as does a natural child. The adopted child has no right to inherit from his natural parents, with the exception of the natural parent who is married to the adoptive parent. For example, if a child loses a parent and is later adopted by a step-parent, the child has the right to inherit from his natural parents and their respective families, and from his adoptive parent as well (ORC 3107.15).

THE ADOPTED ADULT

The rights of a person who is adopted as an adult differs from that of a minor child. Specifically, if a person is adopted after the age of 18, he is not entitled to inherit property from his adoptive parents (nor their relatives) under Ohio's Laws of Descent. This applies to the adopted person's descendants as well. In fact, he (and his descendants) cannot be included as a beneficiary of a Will or Trust unless he is specifically identified as a beneficiary. For example, if his adoptive aunt writes a Will and makes a gift ". . . to my nieces and nephews . . ." the adoptive nephew will not be included in that gift unless the aunt identifies him by name, or states "to my nieces and nephews, including any nephew who was 18 or older when adopted" (ORC 3107.15 (A)(3)).

 **LAWYER** NO SHARE FOR NEGLECTFUL PARENT

Ohio statute does not permit a parent who has neglected to support his minor child to inherit property from that child under the Laws of Descent and Distribution. Specifically, the parent is not entitled to inherit property from a minor child under the age of 18, if, for a year or more prior to the death, the parent:

      ☒   willfully abandoned - or -

      ☒   failed to support the child
          (ORC 2105.10).

Nor can the neglectful parent be compensated for the wrongful death of his child (ORC 2125.02(E)). See Chapter 1 for an explanation of a law suit related to a wrongful death.

The Probate Court is not going to deny a parent's inheritance unless evidence is presented that the parent abandoned or neglected to support his minor child. If you believe that a parent is not entitled to inherit the child's property under Ohio law, you need to employ an attorney who is experienced in Probate litigation to present such evidence to the Court.

HOW TO READ THE WILL

If the decedent left a Will, then the Will states who is to receive the property. Most Wills are short and easy to read, however, you may come across an unfamiliar legal term such as the term *per capita*, for example:

> "I leave the rest, residue and remainder of my
> property to my children, Robert, Barry and Carl,
> in equal shares, per capita."

This means that if one child dies before the decedent, then the share intended for that child is to be divided equally between the surviving brothers. This is different than *per stirpes.* If the gift were left to them, in equal shares, per stirpes, and one of them died, the share would go to the children of the deceased child and not to his brothers.

Sometimes a Will is ambiguous and can be read in different ways. In such case, it may be necessary to have the Probate Court decide what the decedent intended.

In the next section, we examine different problems that can arise with the Will and when to consider challenging the validity of the Will.

CHALLENGING THE WILL

It is not uncommon for a family member to be unhappy with the way the decedent willed his property. If you are tempted to challenge a Will, first consider whether the Will is valid under Ohio law.

Ohio statute requires that the Will be in writing and signed by the person who is making the Will, in the presence of two witnesses, who saw him sign the Will, or heard him say that he was signing his Will (ORC 2107.03).

In Ohio, a Will is presumed to be valid if at the time the decedent made the Will:

➢   he was at least 18 years of age, and

➢   he was of sound mind and memory, and

➢   he was not under restraint (ORC 2107.02).

Ohio Courts have ruled that a person is thought to have acted with sound mind and memory provided:

☑   he knew what he was doing, namely making a Will, and

☑   he knew what property he owned, and

☑   he remembered the names and identities of his family members, and

☑   he understood his relation to the members of his family (*Kata* v. *Second National Bank*, 271 N.E.2d 292 (Ohio, 1971)).

| ☒ | THE WILL WITNESSED BY A BENEFICIARY |

Each person who signs as witness to a Will needs to be at least 18 (ORC 2107.06). Neither of the witnesses of the decedent's Will should be a beneficiary of the Will. Under Ohio law, a gift made to a witnesses to the Will is *void*, meaning that the witness has no legal right to that gift, unless:

⇨ there are two other independent witnesses - or -

⇨ the witness is the decedent's heir under the
   Ohio Laws of Descent.

A Will is not invalid because a beneficiary of the Will, witnesses the Will. It just means that the beneficiary is not entitled to receive that gift, unless one of the above exceptions are met. If the witness is an heir under Ohio's Laws of Descent, he may take so much of the gift as he would have received had the decedent died without a Will (ORC 2107.15).

| ☒ | UNDUE INFLUENCE |

The reason Ohio law prohibits a beneficiary of the Will to be a witness to the Will is that of **undue influence**. Ohio Courts have ruled that undue influence occurs if:

➢ the Will maker is susceptible to being influenced
   by another, and

➢ someone had an opportunity to exert pressure
   on the Will maker (such as being present
   when the Will was signed), and

➢ and in fact improper influence was exerted
   or attempted, and

➢ the Will showed the effect of such influence
   (*Krishbaum v. Dillion*, 567 N.E.2d 1291 (Ohio, 1991)).

These are not easy things to prove. But if the Court finds there was undue influence, the entire Will may be declared invalid and the decedent's property distributed according to Ohio's Laws of Descent and Distribution.

☒   THE VERBAL WILL

Picture a death bed scene. The elderly gentleman is surrounded by several family members. In a whisper, just audible enough to be heard, he says: "Even though I am a wealthy man, I never got around to making a Will. You all have been good to me, but I did want my entire fortune to go to my nephew, Robert. He has been like a son to me. "

Do you think Robert can inherit his Uncle's Estate?

If this took place in the state of Ohio, Robert might be in luck provided:

⇨   Within 10 days, someone writes down his uncles's last wishes, and two competent, disinterested, witnesses sign the writing, AND

⇨   The witnesses testify that when the uncle expressed his wishes, he was of sound mind and memory and under no restraint. In other words, he knew what he was doing and no one was forcing him to make a Will, AND

⇨   The witnesses testify that the uncle called on someone to bear witness that this was his Will (ORC 2107.60).

Robert would need to be extraordinarily lucky if all this takes place considering that, in the absence of a Will, the family members would probably inherit the uncle's fortune under Ohio's Laws of Descent.

Even if the Will is allowed, Ohio statute allows a verbal Will for personal property, only. If the uncle owned real property in the state of Ohio, his real property is inherited by his next of kin as determined by the Ohio Laws of Descent (ORC 2107.60).

CHALLENGING THE WILL

If you can prove the decedent was under 18 when he signed the Will, you have it made. Challenging the Will on other grounds may be difficult — especially if the Will was prepared by the decedent's attorney, who will, no doubt, testify that the Will maker's mind was perfectly clear when he signed the document; and that he signed it of his own free will.

But difficult is not impossible as we will see on the next page. If you are concerned about the validity of the Will, it is important to consult with an attorney experienced in Probate litigation.

Sometimes a person who is of sound mind, makes a Will, but that Will has the effect of giving a spouse or a minor child less than is required under Ohio law. One such example is that of Nancy. Hers was not an easy life. She worked long hours as a waitress. She divorced her hard drinking first husband. The final judgment gave her their home, some securities, and sole custody of their son. After the divorce, Nancy had her attorney prepare a Will leaving all she owned to her son, Richard.

Some years later she met and married Harry, a chef at the restaurant where she worked. He moved into her home and they later had a daughter. Richard was 19, and his half-sister 12, when Nancy died after a lengthy battle with cancer.

Nancy did not leave much — her car, her home, and the securities now worth about $100,000, all in Nancy's name only. Before she died, she told Richard that she had not changed her Will because she wanted him to have all she owned. She said Harry had a good job and she was sure he would take good care of their daughter.

No sooner was the funeral over, when Harry's stepson came in and demanded that Harry vacate his mother's home and give him the keys to her car. Harry was furious and went to his attorney.

"I was a good husband to Nancy, supporting and taking care of her all during her long illness. It was me, and not her son who was at her side when she died. "Now Richard is demanding that I get out of the house and give him the keys to her car. Can he do that to me? Don't I have Curtesy rights or something?"

"Curtesy rights were abolished in Ohio back in 1953 (ORC 2103.09). However, Dower rights were extended to both husband and wife. Each has the right to a Life Estate in one-third of the property owned by his spouse during the marriage. Once a partner dies, the Dower rights are replaced by the **Elective Share** (ORC 2106.01). You can elect to take whatever she left to you under her Will (in this case, nothing) or what you would have inherited had she died without a Will — provided you did not disclaim any of these rights (ORC 5815.34). Did you sign any document such as an *Antenuptial* (i.e., Premarital) Agreement or a separate disclaimer of your marital rights?

"No, I didn't sign anything."

"Then you are entitled to an intestate share of Nancy's Estate. Because Nancy had one child not yours, and another with you, your share is equal the first $60,000, plus one third of the balance. Nancy's children will share the remaining two-thirds (ORC 2105.06)."

"Is that what my daughter inherits?"

"Yes. Your daughter was born after your wife made her Will. Unless Nancy made some provision for her child, her daughter is entitled to inherit as much as she would have inherited if her mother died without a Will (ORC 2107.34). In other words, she is entitled to inherit the same amount as her half-brother."

"What about the car? I need that car to get to work."

"Ohio statute 2106.18 provides that unless Nancy made a specific gift of the car to someone as part of her Will or through joint ownership of the car with another, or if she made Transfer On Death arrangements, you have the right to take the car as part of your inheritance."

"And the house. Do I have to move out?"

"Under Ohio laws, unless your wife's Will makes a specific gift of the house to someone, you have the right to take the home as part of your Elective Share, or you can buy the house, and all of its household goods (ORC 2106.10, 2106.16).

"But the house has appreciated so much that it costs more than I inherit. I can't afford to buy it."

"In such case, under Ohio law, you can continue to live there free of charge for one year (ORC 2106.15). You and your daughter are allowed a Support Allowance of up to $40,000. That $40,000 comes right off the top, free of any creditor claims, and it is not counted as part of your inheritance or part of your daughter's inheritance (ORC 2106.13)."

"Sound's good to me. I'll take the car, the year in the house, $40,000 as a Support Allowance, my inheritance of $60,000 and one-third of whatever is left."

"Not so fast. All of this is subject to Court approval. Once the Will is filed with the Court and an inventory is taken, the Probate court will issue a citation to you giving you thirty days to make your Election (ORC 2106.01 (E))."

The judge awarded Harry the car and $20,000 as a Support Allowance for him and his daughter. He ruled that Harry had the right to continue to live in the home for a year without charge, and that he and his daughter each had the right to an intestate share of the Estate.

Richard did not fare as well as his mother intended. Richard's inheritance was diminished by the share given to his stepfather and to his half sister (ORC 2107.55). The stock had to be sold to pay for the cost of Administration, his mother's burial and funeral, the Family Allowance and Harry's $60,000. All that Richard inherited was his one-third share of the house. And he didn't get that until the house was sold at the end of the year.

No doubt Nancy did not understand what would happen to her Estate once she passed on. The Will she left did not accomplish her goal of providing for her son. All it did was cause turmoil and an irreparable rift between Harry and Richard. It didn't need to be that way. Had Nancy known about Ohio law, she could have consulted with an attorney and set up an Estate Plan that could have provided for her son without alienating her husband.

But the moral of the story, for the purpose of this discussion, is that if you believe that the decedent's Will is not valid or is not drafted according to Ohio law, consult with an attorney experienced in Probate matters to determine your legal rights under that Will.

Getting Possession Of The Property 6

Knowing who is entitled to receive the decedent's property is one thing. Getting that property is another. As explained in the previous chapter, if the decedent owned property Jointly With Right of Survivorship, or In Trust For someone, the property now belongs to the joint owner or beneficiary of the Trust.

As explained in Chapter 4, if the decedent owned a joint bank account, the surviving joint owner is free to withdraw all of the money in the account — understanding that taxes may be due on the inheritance of the decedent's share of the account.

If the decedent owned real or personal property in his name only, or if he owned property as a Tenant In Common, some sort of Probate procedure will be necessary in order to transfer ownership to the proper beneficiary. This chapter describes the different kinds of Probate procedures that are available in Ohio and when it is appropriate to use that procedure.

You may need to employ an attorney should Probate be necessary, but there are many items that can be transferred without the need for Probate. This chapter explains how to get possession of those items.

DISTRIBUTING PERSONAL EFFECTS

Too often, the first person to discover the body will help himself to the decedent's *personal effects* (clothing, jewelry, appliances, electrical equipment, cameras, books, stamp or coin collection, household items and furnishing, etc.). Unless that person is the decedent's sole beneficiary, such action is unconscionable, if not illegal.

If the decedent was married and he was without any surviving lineal descendant, all of the decedent's personal effects belong to his spouse unless he left a Will giving a particular item of personal property to someone else. If the decedent was not married, the proper procedure is to give all of his personal effects to the Personal Representative. The Personal Representative has the duty to distribute the property according to the decedent's Will, or if the decedent died without a Will, then according to the Ohio Laws of Intestate Succession.

As discussed on page 109, the spouse and/or minor child are entitled to keep up to $40,000 of the real or personal property free from the claims of the decedent's creditors (ORC 2106.13). The Personal Representative has the duty of delivering to the spouse and/or minor child, whatever items are claimed as Exempt Property.

If Probate is not necessary, the decedent's next of kin, as determined by the Laws of Intestate Succession, need to divide all of the personal effects among themselves in approximately equal proportions. The problem with the term "equal" is that people have different ideas of what "equal" means.

What's Equal?

If the decedent died without a Will, his next of kin may need to take an equal share of the he property. If the decedent had a Will, it may direct his personal property be divided equally between two or more beneficiaries. Unless there is clear evidence that the decedent's Will meant something else, "equal" refers to the monetary value of the item and not to the number of items received. For example, to divide the decedent's personal effects equally, one beneficiary may receive an expensive item of jewelry and another beneficiary may receive several items whose overall value is approximately equal to that single piece of jewelry.

When distributing personal effects there needs to be cooperation and perhaps compromise, or else bitter arguments might arise over items of little monetary value. One such argument occurred when an elderly woman died who was rich only in her love for her five children and ten grandchildren. After the funeral, the children gathered in their mother's apartment. Each child had his/her own furnishings and no need for anything in the apartment. They agreed to donate all of their mother's personal effects to a local charity with the exception of a few items of sentimental value.

Each child took some small item as a remembrance — a handkerchief, a large platter that their mother used to serve family dinners, a doily their mother crocheted. Things went smoothly until it came to her photograph album. Frank, the youngest sibling, said, "I'll take this." Marie objected saying "But there are pictures in that album that I want."

Frank retorted, "You already took all the pictures Mom had on her dresser."

The argument went downhill from there. Unsettled sibling rivalries boiled over, fueled by the hurt of the loss that they were all experiencing. It almost came to blows when the eldest settled the argument:

"Frank, you make copies of all of the photos in the album for Marie. Marie, you make copies of all of the pictures that you took and give them to Frank. This way you both will have a complete set of Mom's pictures. And while you're at it, make copies for the rest of us."

NON-PROBATE TRANSFERS

A *non-Probate transfer* is a transfer of the decedent's property without the need for Probate. For example, if the decedent had a bank account in his name only "In Trust For" someone or with instructions to "Pay On Death" to someone, all the beneficiary need do is produce a death certificate and proper identification to have the money transferred. Securities held jointly with someone, or with instructions to "Transfer On Death" to a named beneficiary, can be transferred to that beneficiary in the same manner (ORC 1109.06, 1109.07, 2131.11).

COMMISSIONER'S CONSENT REQUIRED
Ohio law requires tax clearance for non-Probate transfers. To get the full value of the decedent's property, you will need written permission from the Tax Commissioner. Without such authorization, the financial institution may not dispense with more than three-quarters of the value of the total value of the transfer. Similarly, a financial institution may not pay death benefits, retirement, pension or profit sharing plan in excess of $2,000, without clearance from the Tax Commissioner (ORC 5731.39).

FINAL WAGES

Probate is not required for a family member to take possession of the decedent's final wages, provided those wages do not exceed $2,500. Ohio statute (ORC 2113.04) authorizes the decedent's employer to pay whatever monies are owed to the following family members:

⇨   surviving spouse
⇨   if no spouse, to the decedent's adult children
⇨   if none of these, to the decedent's parent.

But, no matter what the value of the wages, if it later happens that Probate is necessary, the person who accepts the wages may need to turn them over to the Personal Representative, to be included as part of the decedent's Estate.

MOTOR VEHICLE TO SURVIVING SPOUSE

If Probate is not necessary and you are the surviving spouse, you can transfer two cars owned by the decedent's to your name only. You will need to sign an Affidavit described in Ohio Revised Code Section 2106.18 verifying that you have the right to the motor vehicle (ORC 4505.10), i.e., the decedent did not make a gift of his car and its value of the car(s) does not exceed $40,000. You can obtain the Affidavit from the Deputy Registrar's office (ORC 4505.06).

To find the Deputy Registrar's office, look in the government section of the telephone book under CLERK OF COURTS TITLE OFFICE. Some counties list it as the BUREAU OF MOTOR VEHICLES or the AUTO TITLE DEPARTMENT. You can also call the OHIO BUREAU OF MOTOR VEHICLES for information at (614) 752-7500 or visit their Web site.

OHIO BUREAU OF MOTOR VEHICLES
http://www.bmv.ohio.gov/

MOTOR VEHICLE TO JOINT OWNER OR TOD BENEFICIARY

Probate is not necessary if title to the decedent's car was held Jointly With Right of Survivorship or if title to the car has a Transfer On Death ("TOD") designation to a named beneficiary. The surviving joint owner or TOD beneficiary can go to the County Title office in the Court of Common Pleas to transfer title to his name only (ORC 2106.17).

The TOD beneficiary will need to obtain his own registration from the Deputy Registrar's office (ORC 4505.10). Some counties require a tax release from the County Auditor, so you might save time if you first call your local Deputy Registrar's Office. Ask for the location of the Deputy Registrar's office nearest you, what documents they require and the cost of the transfer.

BOAT TO SPOUSE/JOINT OWNER /TOD BENEFICIARY

As with a motor vehicle, a new title certificate may be issued to the surviving spouse or to the joint owner of a boat or to a named Transfer On Death beneficiary. If the decedent did not make a gift of the boat, his surviving spouse may take title to the decedent's boat and/or outboard motor by signing an Affidavit with the Clerk of the Court of Common Pleas verifying that the decedent did not make a gift of the boat or outboard motor (ORC 2106.19, 2131.12, 2131.13).

If Probate is necessary, it becomes the job of the Personal Representative to transfer the car to the proper beneficiary. If the Will makes a *specific gift* of the car, the Personal Representative will transfer the car to that person. If the decedent did not make a specific gift of his car, his surviving spouse has the right to two of the decedent's cars, provided the appraised value of the car(s) is not more than $40,000.

DETERMINING THE VALUE OF THE CAR

Cars are valued in different ways. The *collateral* value of the car is the value that banks use to evaluate the car for purposes of making a loan to the owner of the car. If you were to trade in a car for the purpose of purchasing a new one, the car dealer would offer you its *wholesale* value. Were you to purchase that same car from a car dealer, he would price it at its *retail* or *fair market value*. Usually the retail price is highest, wholesale is lowest and its collateral value is somewhere in between.

You can call your local bank to get the collateral value of the car. It may be more difficult to obtain the wholesale value because the amount of money a dealer is willing to pay depends on the value of the new car that you are purchasing. You can determine the car's retail value by looking at comparable used car advertisements in the local newspaper. Rather than going through the effort of determining these three values, you can use your Internet search engine to look up the Kelly Blue Book Value. The Web site gives Low, Average and High Blue Book Values which correspond to the wholesale, collateral and retail values.

KELLY BLUE BOOK
http://www.kbb.com

TRANSFER TO FAMILY, FRIENDS

If there was no mention of the car in the decedent's Will, and the decedent was single, or if married, his spouse does not want the car, it is inherited by the *residuary beneficiaries* under the Will, i.e., those who inherit the *Residuary Estate* (whatever is left once bills, taxes, costs of administration have been paid and special gifts distributed). If the decedent did not have a Will, the car is inherited by the decedent's heirs as determined by Ohio's Laws of Descent and Distribution.

TRANSFER WHEN MORE THAN ONE BENEFICIARY

If there is more than one person who has the right to inherit the car, they all can take title to the car. That may not be a practical thing to do since only one person can drive the car at any given time and if one gets into an accident, they all can be held liable. The better route is for the beneficiaries to agree to have one person take title to the car. The beneficiary who takes the car will be considered to have received that value as part of his inheritance. If none of the beneficiaries want the car, the Personal Representative will sell it and add the proceeds to the amount distributed to the beneficiaries.

It is a good idea to limit the use of the car until it is sold or transferred to the beneficiary. If the decedent's car is involved in an accident before the car is transferred to the new owner, the decedent's Estate may be liable for the damage. Having adequate insurance on the car may save the Estate from monetary loss, but a pending lawsuit could delay Probate and prevent any money from being distributed to the beneficiaries until the lawsuit is settled.

CANCELING THE DRIVER'S LICENSE & VOTER REGISTRATION

It is important to notify the Bureau of Motor Vehicles of the death by giving them a certified copy of the death certificate. You can turn in the decedent's driver's license or photo identification card record at the same time title to the car is transferred. If the decedent was disabled and had a parking placard, it needs to be returned as well. The Registrar of Motor Vehicles assists in making changes to voter registration (ORC 3503.11). You can ask them to have the county Board of Elections remove the decedent's name from the list of voters. This helps the Bureau of Motor Vehicles and the Board of Elections in preventing others from using the decedent's name for fraudulent purposes.

TRANSFERRING THE LEASED CAR

The leased car is not an asset of the Estate because the decedent did not own the car. He was obligated to pay the balance of the monies owed on the lease agreement, so the car is a liability to the Estate. The Personal Representative needs to work out an agreement with the company to either assign the lease to someone who agrees to pay the balance of the lease — or have the Estate pay off the lease by purchasing the car under the terms of the lease.

If the remaining payments exceed the current market value of the car, there may be a temptation to hand the keys over to the leasing company. This may not be the best strategy. The leasing company can sell the car and then sue the Estate for the balance of the money owed. If the decedent had no assets or if his only assets are creditor proof, simply returning the car may be an option. But if the decedent's Estate has assets available to pay the balance of the lease payments, the Personal Representative needs to arrange to have the car transferred in a way that releases the Estate from all further liability.

TRANSFERRING SNOWMOBILES/ALL-PURPOSE VEHICLES

The Personal Representative will transfer title to the beneficiary of decedent's snowmobile, off-highway motorcycle, or all-purpose vehicle. If you are the beneficiary of such vehicle, and you plan to operate it exclusively on your own land, then you do not need to register it (ORC 4519.02). However, if you intend to operate the vehicle on public lands, you will need to file an application for registration with Registrar of Motor Vehicles (ORC 4519.03). You can call the Bureau of Motor Vehicles at (614) 752-7500 for the location of the Registrar of Motor Vehicles nearest you.

TRANSFERRING WATERCRAFT

All motor boats used primarily in the state of Ohio must be titled with the Title Office located in the Court of Common Pleas, and registered with the Ohio Department of Natural Resources. The Personal Representative will transfer title to the boat to the proper beneficiary. If you are the new owner of the boat, you will need to obtain your own registration within 45 days of the transfer (ORC 1547.531).

Watercraft Agents are in charge of issuing boat registrations. You can call the Department of Natural Resources for the registration office nearest you. In Ohio, call (877) 426-2837. Out of state, call (614) 265-6480.

You can get information about boat registration, and a list of registration agents and their offices, at the Ohio Department of Natural Resources Web site.

 OHIO DEPARTMENT OF NATURAL RESOURCES
http://www.ohiodnr.com/watercraft

A mobile home that is motorized and not permanently attached to real property is considered to be personal property. Like any motor vehicle, it is titled and registered with the Bureau of Motor Vehicles. The beneficiary of the motorized mobile home will need to have it titled and registered as described earlier in the Chapter.

A mobile or manufactured home that is used for residential purposes and permanently attached to the land, or connected to utility, water, or sewerage facilities is considered to be an improvement to real property. As with any other house on a parcel of land, it is assessed and taxed by the County Auditor (ORC 4503.061).

If the decedent was renting space in a trailer park, the new owner needs to sign a lease agreement with the trailer park owner.

If the decedent owned the land under the mobile home, the house and the land need to be transferred to the proper beneficiary. Title to the home is transferred as personal property. Title to the land is transferred as described later in this chapter.

Hopefully, the beneficiary of the home and the beneficiary of the land are the same person. If not, the beneficiary of the mobile/manufactured home will need a lease agreement with the beneficiary of the land. If the beneficiary of the land refuses to lease the space, the beneficiary of the mobile/manufactured home will need to relocate the home to a trailer park, or perhaps to a parcel of land that he may decide to purchase.

TRANSFERRING AIRCRAFT

If the decedent owned an aircraft, the Personal Representative will need to arrange to transfer title to the proper beneficiary. The new owner of the airplane will need to register it with both the FAA and with the Ohio Office of Aviation.

FAA REGISTRATION

If you are the new owner of the decedent's aircraft you need to register it with the **FAA AIRCRAFT REGISTRATION BRANCH.** You will need to pay the registration fee and:

⇨　complete an **Aircraft Registration Application (AC FORM 8050-1),**

⇨　show proof of ownership, such as a bill of sale

Call the Registration Branch at (405) 954-3116 or toll free (866) 762-9434 for a copy of the Registration Application or download the form from the FAA Website.

http://www.faa.gov/

OHIO REGISTRATION

The Ohio Director of Transportation is in charge of the registration for aircraft based within the state. If you are the new owner of the aircraft and intend to base your plane in Ohio, you need to apply for your own registration within 30 days of the transfer (ORC 4561.18, 4561.20).

You can obtain registration forms from your local airport manager, or by calling the **OHIO OFFICE OF AVIATION** at (614) 387-2354.

You can download registration forms and get many of your questions related to operating an aircraft within Ohio answered from the Department of Transportation Web site.

 OHIO DEPARTMENT OF TRANSPORTATION
http://www.dot.state.oh.us/Aviation

THE FEDERAL INCOME TAX REFUND

Any refund due to the decedent under a joint federal income tax return filed by his surviving spouse will be sent to the surviving spouse. If the decedent's Personal Representative filed the final return, the refund check will be sent to him to be deposited to the Estate account.

If the decedent was single and no Probate proceeding is necessary, whoever is entitled to the decedent's Estate is entitled to the refund check. If you are the beneficiary of the decedent's Estate, you can obtain the refund by filing IRS form 1310 along with the decedent's final income tax return (the 1040).

You can obtain form 1310 from the decedent's accountant, or if he did not have an accountant and you wish to file yourself, you can call the IRS at (800) 829-3676 to obtain the form.

You can download instructions, publications and forms from the Internal Revenue Service by going to the **FORMS AND PUBLICATIONS** section of their Website.
http://www.irs.gov/

The Personal Representative does not need to file form 1310 because once he files the decedent's final income tax return, any refund will be forwarded to him. Similarly, it is not necessary for the surviving spouse who filed a joint return to file form 1310.

If you have not yet received the refund, you can check on it by calling (800) 829-4477, or by visiting the IRS Web site.

THE OHIO INCOME TAX REFUND

As explained in Chapter 2, the decedent's final Ohio income tax return needs to be filed at the same time the federal income tax return is filed, namely by April 15th of the year following the death (ORC 5747.08). If the decedent was married, his surviving spouse can file a joint return. If Probate is necessary, the Personal Representative is responsible for filing final tax income tax returns. If Probate is not necessary, whoever takes possession of the decedent's property needs to file the final return.

DEPOSITING THE TAX REFUND

If the decedent was not married, and the Personal Representative filed the final return, the refund check will be sent to him to be deposited into the Estate account. If a Personal Representative has not yet been appointed, the refund check (or any other check) in the name of the decedent, can be deposited into the decedent's bank account. You can get the money in the decedent's account by using whichever Probate procedure is appropriate.

TRANSFERRING REAL PROPERTY

Probate is not necessary to transfer real property located in Ohio if the property was titled in any of the following ways:

LIFE ESTATE: the decedent was the owner of a Life Estate

SURVIVORSHIP DEED: the decedent owned the property jointly with right of survivorship

TENANTS BY ENTIRETY: the property was transferred before 4/4/85 and was owned by the decedent and his surviving spouse as Tenants by the Entirety

TRANSFER ON DEATH DEED: the deed was in the decedent's name with instruction to Transfer On Death to a named beneficiary.

In each of these cases, the surviving Grantee(s) own the property as of the date of death. Nothing needs to be done to establish that ownership, but the decedent's name remains on the deed. The death certificate is not part of the public record, so anyone examining title to the property will not know of the death (ORC 5302.17).

For taxing purposes and to give notice that the surviving owner now has full authority to possess and/or transfer the property, an Affidavit and a certified copy of the death certificate need to be recorded with the County Auditor and the County Recorder. Ohio statute describes the information that needs to be included in the Affidavit (see ORC 5309.081 for a Survivorship Deed and 5302.22 for a Transfer on Death Deed). However it is best to seek the counsel of an attorney to be sure that the document is prepared and signed according to Ohio law.

It will take a Probate procedure to transfer property owned by the decedent in his name only, or as a Tenant in Common. As part of the Probate proceedings, the Personal Representative will file an application requesting the Probate court to issue a *Certificate of Transfer* to distribute the decedent's real property. The Court will set a hearing on the matter. Anyone who may have an interest in the property will be given notice of the time and place of the hearing (ORC 2113.61).

The Personal Representative will have the County Recorder record the Certificate Of Transfer in the same book as is used to record deeds. The County Recorder will list the name of the decedent as the Grantor and the name of the person who inherits the property as the Grantee (ORC 2113.61, 2113.62). Once the Certificate is recorded, the Grantee is free to occupy or transfer the property.

TRANSFER UNDER TORREN'S SYSTEM

As explained in Chapter 3, a parcel of land may be registered with the Court under the Torrens System, however it takes a Court procedure to have the property titled in the name of a new owner. If you inherit a property registered under the Torrens System, you can have your attorney register the property with the Court in your name, or you can opt out of the Torrens System by asking the Court to have the land recorded in the same manner as unregistered land, namely, with the County Recorder (ORC 5309.68).

Special Situation

TRANSFERRING OUT OF STATE PROPERTY

Each state regulates the transfer of real property within that state. Many states do not require any document be recorded to transfer real property to a surviving joint tenant who has a right of survivorship, or to the owner of the remainder interest of a Life Estate. All the Grantee needs to do is keep a certified copy of the death certificate to produce at closing when the property is sold or transferred. Other states may require the recording of an Affidavit of Survivorship. You can call the recording department in the county where the property is located to find out what documents (if any) need to be recorded to let people know that the surviving Grantee now owns the property. In Ohio, the County Recorder is in charge of recording deeds (ORC 2113.62). In other states, it might be the Clerk of the Circuit Court, or the County Registrar.

Of course, if the decedent owned real property in his own name or as a Tenant In Common, you need to contact an attorney in that state to have the property transferred to the proper beneficiary.

Suppose that the decedent had his affairs arranged so that the only thing he had in his name was a stock worth $25,000. Or maybe all he left was a house worth $75,000 that goes to his spouse. The state of Ohio recognizes that, in certain situations, property can (and should) be transferred to the proper beneficiary quickly and without the need for a full and costly Probate procedure. The Court will allow a **Release From Administration** in each of the following situations:

⇨ The value of the Probate Estate is $100,000 or less and the spouse is the only beneficiary of the Estate.

⇨ The value of the Probate estate is $35,000 or less (regardless of who is the beneficiary of the Estate).

If either of these apply, the Court can issue an order directing that the property be released to the proper beneficiary. The Court will not issue the order unless:

☑ Someone files an application to have the Estate released from administration.

☑ If there is a Will, it has been admitted to Probate.

☑ Notice of the application is delivered to the spouse or other heirs as directed by the Court.

☑ Notice has been published in the newspaper if directed by the Court.

☑ An appraisal of the property is either performed or excused by the Court.

☑ The Court determines that it is proper to release the Estate from any further administration (ORC 2113.03).

As you can see, much of the Probate Procedure still needs to be done before the Court will allow a Release From Administration. In most cases, you will need an attorney to help you through the process.

THE FULL PROBATE PROCEDURE

There needs to be a full Probate proceeding if the decedent left property in his name only or as a Tenant In Common; worth more than $35,000, or $100,000 if the surviving spouse is the sole beneficiary. The proceeding can take anywhere from several months to more than a year depending on the size and complexity of the Probate Estate. A Personal Representative must be appointed and Letters issued.

APPOINTING THE PERSONAL REPRESENTATIVE

Ohio statute gives an order of priority in the appointment of a Personal Representative. Whoever the decedent named as Personal Representative or Executor of his Will has top priority. If that person is unable or unwilling to serve, the person named in the Will as alternate Personal Representative has priority. Ohio statute gives the Will maker the right to name someone to choose who will serve as Personal Representative. If so, whoever is named by that person has priority to serve (ORC 2107.65).

If the decedent died without a Will, the surviving spouse has the right to be appointed Personal Representative. If the spouse is unable or unwilling to serve, or if the decedent was single, anyone who has the right to inherit under Ohio's Laws of Descent and Distribution can be appointed (ORC 2113.06).

Whoever wishes to serve as Personal Representative must be a resident of Ohio. If not, the judge may require assurances from the Personal Representative that all of the Probate assets will remain in the county until they are distributed. The Court may also require the appointment of a resident ancillary (secondary) Personal Representative who can share the administrative duties with the non-resident Representative (ORC 2109.21)

YOUR RIGHTS AS A BENEFICIARY

The Personal Representative is in charge of settling the Estate. Too often, beneficiaries of the Estate have no idea what is going on. They wait to receive their inheritance, not knowing that they have rights under Ohio law; and more importantly, not knowing how to assert their rights.

✧ **RIGHT TO BE KEPT INFORMED**

You, as a beneficiary of the decedent's Estate, have the right to be kept informed of the progress of the Probate procedure. Unless you waive (give up) your right to be notified, within two months of his appointment, the Personal Representative is required to give you written notice of his appointment (ORC 2107.19). Once you receive this notice, write to him (with a copy to his attorney) requesting that he provide you with a copy of all documents that he files with the Court, beginning with a copy of the Will (if any).

✧ **RIGHT TO YOUR OWN ATTORNEY**

The attorney who handles the Estate is employed by, and represents, the Personal Representative. If the Estate is sizeable, consider employing your own attorney to check that things are done properly and in a timely manner. Even if the Estate is small, consider consulting with an attorney any time you are concerned about the way the Probate is being conducted.

✧ **RIGHT TO OBJECT TO PERSONAL REPRESENTATIVE**

Regardless of who has priority to serve, it is the Court who has final say as to who will serve as Personal Representative. The judge can appoint the person with priority, or if the beneficiaries of the Estate object, he can appoint someone who is acceptable to those who have a majority interest in the Estate.

✧   RIGHT TO APPEAR BEFORE THE COURT

You, as a beneficiary, have the right to raise an objection to the appointment of the person who volunteers to be Personal Representative before the Court. However, before doing so, you should consult with an experienced Probate attorney. He can explain the best way for you to present your concerns to the Court. He can tell you what arguments have a good chance of swaying the judge. And he can tell you which arguments have so little probability of success that they are not worth pursuing.

✧   RIGHT TO OBJECT TO THE WILL

The decedent's Will can be admitted into Probate by means of an informal proceeding. You have the right to receive a copy of the Will that is offered for Probate. If you believe the Will is not valid, you can bring your concerns to the attention of the Court, but, again, this is one of those issues that requires the assistance of an experienced Probate attorney. The person who offers the Will into Probate is not about to withdraw that Will without a fight. That fight is called litigation — with the validity of the Will being decided at trial.

✧   RIGHT TO DEMAND BOND

It doesn't happen often, but every now and again a Personal Representative will run off with Estate funds. A bond is insurance for the Estate. If Estate monies are stolen, the company that issued the bond will reimburse the Estate for the loss. It is up to the Court to decide whether a bond is necessary, and if so, the value of the bond (ORC 2109.04, 2109.07). In general, the Court will not order a bond if the Personal Representative is an authorized bank or trust company or if the spouse is Personal Representative and sole beneficiary of the Estate.

If the decedent's Will says that no bond should be required, the Court can still require a bond if the Court feels that the Estate property needs to be protected (ORC 2109.04). Most Wills state that no bond shall be required. The reason is two-fold. The Will maker chooses someone he trusts to administer the Estate, so he does not think bond is necessary. And there are economic reasons. The cost of the bond is paid for by the Estate, and ultimately the amount inherited is reduced by the amount paid for the bond. For that reason, beneficiaries of the Estate can file a waiver asking the Court to dispense with the bond requirement.

The cost of the bond should not be a factor if there is any danger of the Estate property being lost or mismanaged. If you are concerned about the safety of the Estate assets, it is important that you not sign a waiver, but rather ask the Court to order the Personal Representative to be bonded. The value of the bond should be at least twice the value of the decedent's personal property. Once you have a copy of the inventory, check to see if there is sufficient bond. If not, you can ask the court to have the bond increased (ORC 2109.06).

✧ RIGHT TO KNOW PERSONAL REPRESENTATIVE'S FEES

The Personal Representative is entitled to be compensated for his efforts in settling the Estate. If he is also a beneficiary of the Estate he may decide not to take a *commission* (i.e., fee) and just take his inheritance. The reason may be economic. Inherited funds are not considered to be income to the beneficiary, so there is no federal or state income tax on those monies. Any fee the Personal Representative takes is taxable as ordinary income, but monies he inherits is not taxable to him as a beneficiary. Ask the Personal Representative to tell you, in writing, whether he intends to charge a fee, and if so, how much.

There are statutory guidelines for what is "reasonable" compensation. The Personal Representative is entitled to a percentage of the decedent's personal property, including income from the personal property that is received by the Personal Representative:

> 4% on the first $100,000
> 3% on the next $300,000
> 2% on the balance.

He is allowed a commission of 1% of the fair market value the decedent's real property. The Personal Representative is also entitled to 1% of property that is not subject to Probate, but included as part of the decedent's Ohio Estate Tax return — with the exception of joint and survivorship property (ORC 2113.35). The Court can increase the amount due to the Personal Representative for any extraordinary service performed in settling the Estate (ORC 2113.36).

✧ RIGHT TO KNOW THE ATTORNEY'S FEES

The job of administering the decedent's Estate is complex and there is potential liability associated with it. The Personal Representative must settle the Estate by paying all valid claims, taxes and costs of Administration. Monies are paid from the decedent's Estate and not from the Personal Representative's pocket. However, if he makes a mistake, he may be responsible to pay for that mistake. For example, suppose the Personal Representative pays a debt that did not need to be paid, or doesn't pay a claim that needed to be paid. In such cases, the Personal Representative may be responsible to pay for such error (ORC 2113.53). He may be personally liable to pay for taxes on the transfer of the decedent's property if he neglect to collect taxes from the person who is responsible to pay those taxes (ORC 5731.37)

The Personal Representative has the right to employ an attorney to guide him through the Probate procedure so that things will be done properly and at no personal cost to the Representative. It is proper to have the attorney paid with Estate funds. You, as a beneficiary of the Estate, have the right to know how much will be charged for legal fees. Ask the Personal Representative to give you a copy of the retainer agreement. If the attorney is employed on an hourly basis, have the attorney give a written estimate of the time he expects to spend on the Probate proceeding.

There is no statutory guideline for what is a "reasonable" fee for the attorney. The attorney's fees are set by the Court, but you can expect they will be at least as much as those of the Personal Representative (ORC 2113.36). If you think the fees being charged are unreasonable, you can call different law firms and ask what they charge to Probate an Estate with similar assets. That will give you some idea of the going rate. If after doing some "comparison shopping" you still believe that the attorney is charging too much, you can negotiate with them to lower the fee. If you cannot reach an agreement, you can ask the Probate Court to set a hearing to settle the matter.

✦ RIGHT TO COPY OF INVENTORY

The Personal Representative must prepare an inventory of all of the assets of the Probate Estate. Within three months of his appointment, he must file the inventory with the Court, together with an appraisal of the assets of the Estate (ORC 2115.02). The Court will set a hearing to approve the inventory. Unless you waived your right, you should be given notice of the hearing, either by the Court or the Personal Representative (ORC 2115.16). It is important that you review the appraisal and inventory because the values are used to determine the Personal Representative's fees, how much taxes need to be paid, and ultimately how much you will receive.

If you believe that some item was omitted from the inventory or was not appraised correctly, you can raise an objection with the Court. You will need to file your objection at least five days before the hearing (ORC 2115.16).

Recall that, under Ohio law, a car, boat or outboard motor taken by the surviving spouse as part of her Exempt Property is not included as part of the Estate inventory, so these are not missing inventory items (ORC 2106.18, 2106.19). See Chapter 4.

✧   RIGHT TO AN ACCOUNTING

Unless the Estate is subject to Estate Taxes, or there is some problem with settling the Estate, such as a challenge to the Will, the Personal Representative will file a Final Accounting within six months from the date of his appointment (ORC 2109.301). He is required to send a copy of the account to each beneficiary of the Estate.

The accounting begins with the inventory value of the Estate and ends with the value of the property on hand. The amount on hand in the Final Accounting is the amount that will be distributed to the beneficiaries of the Estate. If the Estate has a significant amount of assets, you may wish to have your own accountant or attorney look over the accounting. Each accounting must be approved by the Court. The Court will schedule a hearing on the accounting. If you have any question or objection to the accounting you can raise those issues at the Court hearing (ORC 2109.32).

The Personal Representative, or his attorney, may ask you to sign a waiver of your right to an accounting (ORC 2109.301). But keep in mind that the accounting is for your benefit. There are few situations that justify you giving up your right to know how Estate monies were spent.

✧ RIGHT TO HAVE THE ESTATE CLOSED WITHOUT DELAY

How long it takes to complete the Probate proceeding depends on the size and complexity of the Estate. The Personal Representative can close out the Estate anytime after the time allowed for creditors to come forward and present a claim. Generally, that is six months from the date of death (ORC 2117.06). The Personal Representative may want to wait a year before he closes the Estate because, under Ohio law, he, and the beneficiaries, can be held personally liable to anyone who suffers a loss if he closes the Estate before a year has passed (ORC 2113.53).

It may take longer than a year to close the Estate, if an Estate Tax return has been filed. However, you should expect the Estate to be closed within 90 days of the receipt of the federal and state tax release. If you do not receive an accounting and a proposed plan of distribution within these time periods, you have the right to ask the Court to order the Personal Representative to distribute your share of the Estate to you (ORC 2113.54).

✧ RIGHT TO RECEIVE A DEBT FREE INHERITANCE

Once a beneficiary finally receives his inheritance, about the last thing he wants to hear is that there is some unfinished business, or worse yet that monies need to be paid from the inheritance he received. But that is just what could happen if the Personal Representative distributes the Estate before all valid claims are paid (ORC 2117.41). As explained on Page 99, a creditor who is given notice of the death must file a claim within 30 days of the notice (ORC 2117.07) If the Estate is being closed before the year is out, ask the Personal Represntative whether he gave written notice to all known creditors. And if not, whether he is aware of any outstanding debts.

Taxes are another concern. You should ask to see a copy of all of the tax returns that were filed, and then verify that any money that was due has been paid. If the Personal Representative fails to file a return, or fails to pay taxes, or if he under-reports a tax obligation, you could later be called on to pay Estate Taxes out of the proceeds you receive as a beneficiary of the Estate (ORC 2117.41).

IT'S YOUR RIGHT - DON'T BE INTIMIDATED

You may feel uncomfortable being assertive with a friend or family member who is Personal Representative. Don't be. It's your money and your right to be informed. Be especially firm if the Personal Representative waves you off with "You've known me for years. Surely you trust me." People who are trustworthy, don't ask to be trusted. They do what is right. The very fact that the Personal Representative is resisting, is a red flag. In such situation, you can explain that it is not a matter of trust, but a matter of your legal rights.

At the same time, keep things in perspective. Your relationship with the Personal Representative may be more important to you than the money you inherit. The job of settling an Estate can be complex and demanding. If the Personal Representative is getting the job done, let him know you appreciate his efforts.

Once the Probate proceeding is over, you will be left with many documents and wonder which you need to keep:

COURT DOCUMENTS

You should keep a copy of the inventory to establish the value of property that you inherit. That value becomes your basis for any Capital Gains Tax that you may need to pay in the future. Other than the inventory, there is no reason to keep any Court document, provided you are satisfied with the way things were done; and do not intend to take action against the Personal Representative, or his attorney. The Clerk of the Probate Court keeps the Probate file on record, so if for some reason you later need a copy of a Probate document, you can get it from the Clerk.

PERSONAL RECORDS

The surviving spouse, or if no spouse, his next of kin should keep the decedent's personal papers (birth certificate, death certificate, marriage certificate, naturalization papers, army records, religious documents, etc.). They may be needed in order to apply for government, or other, benefits. The next of kin may want to keep the decedent's medical records in the event that a family member needs to check out a genetic disorder.

TAX RECORDS

The IRS has up to three years to collect additional taxes, and you have up to seven years to claim a loss from a worthless security, so you should keep the decedent's tax file for seven years from the date of filing the return. You can learn more about which records to keep from the IRS publication 552. You can get the publication by calling the IRS at (800) 829-3676 or you can download it from their Website: http://www.irs.gov

THE CHECK LIST

We discussed many things that need to be done when some-one dies in the state of Ohio. The next page contains a check list that you may find helpful.

You can check those items that you need to do, and then cross them off the list once they are done. We made the list as comprehensive as possible, so many items may not apply in your case. In such case, you can cross them off the list or mark them *N/A* (not applicable).

Things To Do

FUNERAL ARRANGEMENTS TO BE MADE
☐ AUTOPSY ☐ ANATOMICAL GIFT
☐ DISPOSITION OF BODY OR ASHES

DEATH CERTIFICATE
GIVE COPY TO: _____

_____
_____

NOTICE OF DEATH
PEOPLE TO BE NOTIFIED _____

_____

COMPANIES TO NOTIFY
☐ CREDIT CARD COMPANIES
☐ TELEPHONE COMPANY
    ☐ LOCAL CARRIER ☐ LONG DISTANCE   ☐ CELLULAR
☐ NEWSPAPER (OBITUARY PRINTED)
☐ NEWSPAPER DELIVERY CANCELLED   ☐ deposit refund
☐ SOCIAL SECURITY
☐ POWER & LIGHT   ☐ deposit refund
☐ POST OFFICE
☐ OTHER UTILITIES (GAS, WATER)   ☐ deposit refund
☐ PENSION PLAN   ☐ ANNUITY
☐ HEALTH INSURANCE COMPANY
☐ LIFE INSURANCE COMPANY
☐ HOME INSURANCE COMPANY
☐ MOTOR VEHICLE INSURANCE COMPANY
☐ CONDOMINIUM OR HOMEOWNER ASSOCIATION

NOTICE & CANCEL
☐ CANCEL INTERNET SERVER
☐ CANCEL TELEVISION CABLE/SATELLITE COMPANY
☐ CANCEL SERVICE CONTRACT   ☐ deposit refund
☐ CANCEL DRIVER'S LICENSE, OR PHOTO ID
☐ CANCEL VOTER REGISTRATION

Things To Do

REMOVE DECEDENT AS BENEFICIARY OF:

☐ WILL ☐ INSURANCE POLICY ☐ PENSION PLAN
☐ BANK OR IRA ACCOUNT ☐ SECURITIES

DEBTS

PAY DECEDENT'S DEBTS (AMOUNT & CREDITOR)

_____

COLLECT MONIES OWED TO DECEDENT (AMOUNT & DEBTOR)

_____

TAXES

☐ FILE FINAL FEDERAL INCOME TAX RETURN
☐ FILE FINAL OHIO INCOME TAX RETURN
☐ RECEIVE INCOME TAX REFUND
☐ FILE ESTATE TAX RETURN

PROPERTY TO BE TRANSFERRED

☐ PERSONAL EFFECTS
☐ MOTOR VEHICLE
☐ BANK ACCOUNT
☐ CREDIT UNION ACCOUNT
☐ IRA ACCOUNT
☐ SECURITIES
☐ BROKERAGE ACCOUNT
☐ INSURANCE PROCEEDS
☐ HOMESTEAD
☐ TIME SHARE
☐ OTHER REAL PROPERTY
☐ CONTENTS OF SAFE DEPOSIT BOX

OTHER THINGS TO DO

_____
_____
_____

Everyman's Estate Plan 7

The first six chapters of this book describe how to wind up the affairs of the decedent. As you read those chapters, you learned about the kinds of problems that can occur when settling the decedent's Estate. It is relatively simple for you to set up an Estate Plan so that your family members are not burdened with similar problems. An **Estate Plan** is the arranging of your finances for maximum control and protection during your lifetime, and at the same time ensuring that your property will be transferred quickly and at little cost to your heirs.

If you think that only wealthy people need to prepare an Estate Plan, you are mistaken. Each year, heirs of relatively modest Estates, spend thousands of dollars to settle an Estate. A bit of planning could have eliminated most, if not all, of the expense and hassle suffered by those families.

The suggestions in this chapter are designed to assist the average person in preparing a practical and inexpensive Estate Plan, so we named this chapter EVERYMAN'S ESTATE PLAN.

Once you create your own Estate Plan, you can be assured that your family will not be left with more problems than happy memories of you.

AVOIDING PROBATE

After reading the last Chapter, you may come to the conclusion that Probate is a good thing to avoid. Those who have $35,000 or less, or who are married with $100,000 or less going to his/her spouse, may not be concerned with avoiding Probate because the judge may allow a Release From Administration. But as explained, the Court will not allow the Release until much of the Probate procedure is completed (ORC 2113.03). In most cases, your beneficiary will need to employ an attorney to get the judge to agree to the Release From Administration. They will need to pay attorney fees to inherit a relatively small amount of money.

Whatever you own, if property is titled in your name only, a Probate procedure will be necessary with all of its inherent delays and expenses. Notice that the operative phrase in the last sentence is *in your name only*. Whether Probate is necessary depends on how your property is titled (owned). It makes no difference whether you do, or do not, have a Will. If you own property in your name only, and have not made provision for an automatic transfer to a beneficiary, your beneficiary will need to go through Probate in order to take possession of that property.

As explained in Chapter 5, there are many ways to title real property so that it passes automatically without the need for Probate — from a Survivorship Deed, to a Transfer on Death deed, to holding a Life Estate interest. Upon your death, the survivors will own the real property without any need to go through Probate. In this Chapter we examine ways to title your personal property (bank accounts, securities, etc.) so that it passes to your beneficiaries without the need for Probate.

You can arrange to have all of your bank accounts set up so that should you die, the money goes directly to a beneficiary. For example, suppose all you own is a bank account and you want whatever you have in the account to go to your son and daughter when you die. You might think that a simple solution is to put each child's name on the account as Joint Tenants With Right of Survivorship, but first consider the problems associated with a joint account.

⊠ POTENTIAL LIABILITY

If you hold a bank account jointly with your adult child and that child is sued or gets a divorce, the child may need to disclose his ownership of the joint account. In such a case, you may find yourself spending money to prove that the account was established for your convenience only and that all of the money in that account really belongs to you.

⊠ OVERREACHING

If you set up a joint account with your child so that the child has authority to withdraw funds from the account, monies could be withdrawn without your knowledge or consent.

If you have a joint account with two of your children, there is the problem of what happens to the funds after your death. Unless your agreement with the bank states differently, should you die, your *net contribution* to the account, (what you deposited less what you withdrew) should be shared equally by your children. But as a practical matter, each joint owner has free access to the bank account (ORC 1109.07). After your death it could become a race to the bank. If one child withdraws all of the money, that will, at the very least, cause hard feelings between them.

THE BENEFICIARY ACCOUNT

Holding a bank account jointly with a family member eliminates the need for Probate, but at the cost of control of the funds. One way to avoid Probate of the account yet retain full control during your lifetime, is to direct a financial institution to hold your account *In Trust For* (*"ITF"*) one or more beneficiaries that you name. The beneficiary does not have access to that account during your lifetime so an ITF account does not have the potential problem of the joint account, but it does have its Achilles' heel. Namely, under Ohio law, the account is considered to be a Revocable Trust for the beneficiary (ORC 1109.06).

As we will see later in this Chapter, money you put into the Revocable Trust is available to pay your debts, before or after death. If you set up an ITF account, when you die your creditors may say that you were really holding that money in that account as Trustee of a Revocable Trust. On that basis, your creditor might ask the bank to give him the money in the account as payment for your debts.

The bank will not want to get in the middle of an argument between your creditor and the beneficiary of that account so the bank will ask a Probate court to settle the argument. If the purpose of setting up an ITF account is to avoid Probate, then this may not be the best approach for someone who owes significant amounts of money.

There is a better solution to the problem of ensuring your heirs get the money in your bank account without going through Probate and that is direct the bank to **PAYABLE ON DEATH** all of the money in the account to one or more beneficiaries that you name.

THE PAYABLE ON DEATH ACCOUNT

The *Payable On Death* ("P.O.D.") account eliminates the inherent problems of the joint account because the beneficiary does not own any part of the account until the owner of the account dies. Specifically:

⇨   The beneficiary does not have access to the account until the owner of the account dies.

⇨   During his lifetime the owner of the account is free to change beneficiaries without asking the beneficiary's permission to do so (ORC 2131.10).

You can open a P.O.D. account with instructions to the bank to give the money to your child when you die, and if the child dies before you, to your grandchildren in equal shares, per stirpes, The account can be titled:

Eldon Connors P.O.D. Betty Connors LDPS
which is short-hand for:

ELDON CONNORS is the owner of the account. On his death, pay the money in the account to BETTY CONNORS, but if she dies before Eldon, give the money to Betty's lineal descendants, per stirpes.

TRANSFER ON DEATH SECURITIES

The Ohio law for securities is much the same as the statutes for bank accounts. You can arrange to have a security (a stock, bond or brokerage account) transferred to a beneficiary upon your death. You can instruct the holder of the security to Pay On Death or *Transfer On Death* ("TOD") to a named beneficiary (ORC 1709.05).

There may be times when you wish to hold a security jointly (say with your spouse) and have your children inherit the security when you both die. For example:

ELDON CONNORS and LORRAINE CONNORS, JT TEN
TOD FRED CONNORS and MARIE CONNORS

➪ Fred and Marie have no right to the account during the lifetime of their parents.

➪ Should either parent die, the surviving parent owns the account, and is free to close the account or change beneficiaries without asking or telling either of their children (ORC 1709.06).

➪ Should Fred die before his parents and the account is not changed, under Ohio law, the money in the account will go to Marie. Should both Fred and Marie die before their parents, the security will be included in the Estate of the last parent to die (ORC 1709.07).

If your Estate consists only of bank accounts and/or securities, and you want all of your property to go to one or two beneficiaries without the need for Probate, but with maximum control and protection of your funds during your lifetime, then holding your property in any of these beneficiary forms:

In Trust For
Pay On Death
Transfer On Death

should accomplish your goal.

GIFT TO A MINOR CHILD

At the beginning of this chapter, we identified two problems with a joint account: potential liability if the joint owner is sued and overreaching by the joint owner. If you wish to make a gift to a minor child, that presents still another problem. The P.O.D. account and TOD security avoid the problem of potential liability and over-reaching, but if the beneficiary of such account is a minor, there is the problem of the child having access to a large sum of money.

In general, a financial institution will not transfer funds to a minor child without authorization from the Probate Court. If the amount is $10,000 or less, the judge has discretion to transfer the funds to a bank to be kept on deposit until the child is 18, or he can transfer the funds to the child's parents, or even to the child himself (ORC 2111.05).

If the gift is significant in value, the Court will appoint a Guardian to care for the property until the child is grown. But that only presents a new set of problems. It takes time, effort and money to set up a guardianship. The Guardian will need to prepare an inventory of property owned by the minor (ORC 2111.14). The Guardian may need to employ an accountant to submit an accounting of monies spent to the Court. The Guardian, his attorney, the accountant are all entitled to be paid from the child's property. It could happen that the cost of the guardianship significantly reduces the amount of money inherited by the child.

There are ways to avoid the problem of having a Guardian appointed to care for property inherited by a child, and yet ensuring that the monies are protected. One such method is the **OHIO TRANSFERS TO MINORS ACT**.

THE TRANSFERS TO MINORS ACT

The **Ohio Transfers to Minors Act** is designed to protect gifts made to a minor by appointing someone to be the **Custodian** of a gift until the child is an adult. The Custodian can be a trusted friend or relative, or you can name a bank or other financial institution to serve as Custodian. It is appropriate to use the Uniform Transfers To Minors Act if you want to make the child a beneficiary of your Will or of a life insurance policy, or even of a bank account. For example, you can name the bank as Custodian of the bank account in the event that you die before the child is an adult.

> RUSSELL JONES POD FRIENDLY BANK as Custodian For RUSSELL JONES, JR. under the Ohio Transfers to Minors Act (ORC 5814.02).

During your lifetime you are free to deposit or withdraw from the account. You can close the account or change beneficiaries, or even appoint someone else to serve as Custodian of the property.

AGE OF DISTRIBUTION The Custodian must distribute the gift when the child reaches 21; however, you can direct that the gift be given to the child on his attaining any age between 18 and 21. In the above example, no age was mentioned, so should you die before the child is 21, the bank will hold and manage the account until he is 21 (ORC 5814.04).

THE LIFETIME GIFT You can use the Transfers to Minors Act to make gifts during your lifetime such as shares in a corporation. You can nominate yourself as Custodian of the gift, or you can name another person to serve as Custodian. Once the lifetime gift is made it becomes irrevocable, so this method is not appropriate unless you are sure that you want the child to have the gift once he is grown (ORC 5814.03).

The Custodian needs to invest and manage the property in a responsible, prudent manner. He must keep records of all transactions made with custodial property; and make those records available for inspection by the child's parent, or legal representative, or the child, if the minor is 14 or older. If those records are not to their satisfaction, they can petition (ask) the Probate Court to require the Custodian to give an accounting (ORC 5814.08).

The Custodian has the discretion to use the gift to care for the child. The Custodian can pay monies directly to the child, or can use the money for the child's benefit. The Custodian can refuse to use any of the monies for the child and just keep the funds invested until it is time to distribute the funds. If the Custodian wants to keep the funds invested, the child's parent, or the child once he is 14, can ask the Court to order the Custodian to part with some or all of the money for the benefit of the child. The judge will decide what is in the child's best interest and then rule on the matter (ORC 5814.04).

The Custodian is entitled to be paid for his effort each year (ORC 5814.05). If the gift is sizeable, the Custodian's fee can be sizeable. Before appointing a person or a financial institution as Custodian, it is best to come to a written agreement about what will be charged to manage the custodial property.

A gift made under the Ohio Transfers to Minors Act is limited to one minor only. If you want to give a single gift, such as a gift of real property to two or more children or if you want more flexibility about when the minor is to receive the gift, then a Trust may be the better way to go.

We discuss Trusts later in this chapter.

THE GIFT OF REAL PROPERTY

As explained in Chapter 5, if you own real property together with another, then who owns the property upon your death depends on how the Grantee is identified on the face of the deed. If you compare the Grantee clause of the deed to the examples given in Chapter 5 you can determine who will inherit the property when you die. If you are not satisfied with the way the property will be inherited, you need to consult with an attorney to change the deed so that it will conform to your wishes.

If you own the property in your name only or as a Tenant In Common, when you die, there will need to be a Probate proceeding to determine the proper beneficiary of that land. If your main objective is to avoid Probate, you can have an attorney change the deed so that upon your death, the property will descend to your beneficiary without the need for Probate. As with bank and securities accounts there are different ways to do so, each with its own advantages and disadvantages.

JOINT OWNERSHIP

If you hold property in your name only, and wish to avoid Probate, you can have your deed changed so that you and a beneficiary are joint owners with rights of survivorship. If you do so, should either of you die, the other will own the property 100%. That avoids Probate, but by making that person joint owner, you are, in effect, making a gift of half of the property during your lifetime. You will not be able to sell that property without the beneficiary's permission. And if the beneficiary gives permission and the property is sold, the beneficiary will have the legal right to half of the proceeds of the sale.

And you may be creating a Capital Gains Tax problem as well. As explained on page 43, you can arrange to sell your home without paying a Capital Gains Tax, but if you make someone joint owner of your home who does not live with you, a Capital Gains Tax may need to be paid on the joint owner's share of the proceeds should you decide to sell the property.

CAUTION   GIFT OF HOMESTEAD

Some elderly parents worry that they may need nursing care at some time in the future and lose all of their life savings to pay for that care. The parent may decide that the best way to avoid Probate and protect the homestead from loss is to transfer the homestead to their child with the understanding that the parent will continue to live there until he/she dies. But this is just trading risks.

⊠   RISK OF LOSS
Property transferred to your child could be lost if the child runs into serious financial difficulties or is sued. This is especially a risk if your child is a professional (doctor, nurse, accountant, financial planner, attorney, etc.). If your child is (or gets) married, this complicates matters even more. Should the child divorce, the property may need to be included as part of the settlement agreement. This may be to your child's detriment, because the child may need to share the value of the property with his/her former spouse. If you do not transfer the property, it cannot become part of the marital equation.

⊠ LOSS OF HOMESTEAD CREDITOR PROTECTION

As explained in Chapter 4, if you have unpaid medical bills and not enough money in your Estate to pay the debt, the health care provider can place a lien on your home, but if you leave your home to your spouse or minor child, he will not be able to foreclose against the home. The health care provider can collect the debt once the property is sold or transferred to someone other than your spouse or minor child (ORC 2329.66 (A)(1)(a)).

If you transfer your homestead, you lose this protection for your spouse and child.

⊠ LOSS OF HOMESTEAD TAX REDUCTION

If you are receiving a Homestead Tax Reduction and you transfer your home to your child, you may need to pay more in taxes to continue to live in your own home. If you decide to transfer your homestead to a beneficiary, before doing so, call the County Auditor and ask him the tax consequence of such transfer.

⊠ POSSIBLE GIFT TAX

If the value of the transfer is worth more than the Annual Gift Tax Exclusion ($12,000 as of 2006) you need to file a Gift Tax return. For most of us, this is not a problem because no Gift Tax need be paid unless the equity in your home (fair market value less mortgages on the property) plus the value of all gifts in excess of the Annual Gift Tax Exclusion that you gave over your lifetime, exceed $1,000,000 (see Chapter 2). But if your Estate is in that tax bracket, you need to be aware that you are "using up" your lifetime Gift Tax Exclusion.

☒ POSSIBLE CAPITAL GAINS TAX

Although certain members of Congress has expressed a desire to phase out the Estate Tax, there is no discussion to do away with the Capital Gains Tax. If you gift your home to your child during your lifetime, when he sells the property he will pay a Capital Gains Tax on the increase in value from the price you paid for your home to the selling price at the time your child sells the property.

If you do not make the gift during your lifetime, the child will inherit the property with a step-up in basis, i.e., he will inherit the property at its market value as of your date of death. Under today's tax structure and continuing until 2009, that step-up in basis is unlimited. If your child sells the property shortly after he inherits it, he will pay no Capital Gains Tax, regardless of how large the step-up in basis. In 2010, there will be a limit on the amount that can be inherited free of the Capital Gains Tax; but that limit is quite high, so for most of us this is not a concern.

☒ POSSIBLE LOSS OF GOVERNMENT BENEFITS

If you transfer property, you could be disqualified from receiving Medicaid or Supplemental Security Income ("SSI") benefits for a substantial period of time. Under the Deficit Reduction Act that was signed into law on February 8, 2006, whoever applies for Medicaid, must disclose if, within five years of his application, he transferred property for less than the fair market value (i.e., he gifted property). If you apply for Medicaid within five years of the transfer of your home, depending on the value of the transfer, you will be disqualified from receiving Medicaid for a period of time depending on the value of the transfer. The disqualification period begins on the day you apply for Medicaid. This can present a serious problem because you wouldn't be applying unless you were in need of medical assistance.

Unless the equity in your home exceeds $500,000, owning a home will not disqualify you from applying for Medicaid in Ohio (ORC 5111.011, 5111.018). Before transferring your homestead because of your concern for the cost of future health care, consult with an Elder Law attorney. He will be able to suggest ways to protect your assets, and still ensure that you receive the health care that you may require in your later years.

THE PROBLEM OF OUT OF STATE PROPERTY

As explained in Chapter 6, each state is in charge of the way property located in that state is transferred. If you own property in another state (or country), you need to consult with an attorney who practices in that state or country to determine how your property will be transferred to your beneficiaries should you die.

If you own property in another state in your name only, or as a Tenant In Common, or if you hold property with your spouse in a Community Property state, a Probate procedure may need to be held in that state. If it is necessary to have a Probate in Ohio, a second (ancillary) Probate may need to be held in the state where the property is located. This could have the effect of doubling the cost of Probate.

One way to avoid Probate is to title your property so that it is transferred to your beneficiary upon your death, such as Joint Tenants With Right of Survivorship. Another way to avoid the need for Probate, in this or any other state, is to set up a REVOCABLE LIVING TRUST and then place your property into your Trust.

CREATING A TRUST

Probate is necessary if you own property in your name only or as a Tenant In Common. We explored different ways to re-title property to avoid Probate, but these methods have trade-offs that may be unacceptable to you. One way to avoid many of these potential problems is to set up a **Revocable Living Trust** (also known as an *Inter Vivos Trust*).

A Revocable Living Trust is designed to care for your property during your lifetime, and then to distribute your property once you die — without the need for Probate. You may have been encouraged to set up a Trust by your financial planner, attorney, or accountant. Even people of modest means are being encouraged to use a Trust as the basis of their Estate Plan. But Trusts have their pros and cons. Before getting into that, let's first discuss what a Trust is and how it works.

SETTING UP A TRUST

To create a Trust, a person has his attorney prepare a Trust document (a *Trust Agreement*) according to the client's needs and desires. The Agreement is between the person who creates and funds the Trust (the **Settlor** or *Grantor*) and the **Trustee** (manager) of property placed in the Trust. The Settlor usually appoints himself as Trustee so that he is in total control of property he places into the Trust. This means that he signs the Trust Agreement as the Settlor and also as the Trustee who promises to manage the property according to the terms of the Trust Agreement. The Trust document also names a **Successor Trustee** who will take over the management of the Trust property should the Trustee resign, become disabled, or die. We will refer to the Revocable Living Trust as the "Living Trust" or just the "Trust" and the person who creates the Trust as the "Settlor."

Once the Trust Agreement is properly signed, the Settlor transfers property into the Trust. He does this by changing title from his individual name to his name as Trustee. For example, if Elaine Richards sets up a Trust naming herself as Trustee, and she wishes to place her bank account into the Trust, all she need do is instruct the bank to change the name on the account from Elaine Richards to:

ELAINE RICHARDS, TRUSTEE OF THE ELAINE RICHARDS
REVOCABLE TRUST AGREEMENT DATED JULY 12, 2006.

When the change is made, all the money in the account becomes Trust property. Elaine (wearing her Trustee hat) has total control of the account, taking money out, and putting money in, as she sees fit. Similarly, if she wants to put real property into the Trust, she can have her attorney prepare a new deed with the owner identified as ELAINE RICHARDS, TRUSTEE. See page 128 for an example of real property placed into a Trust.

During her lifetime, Elaine is free to *amend* (i.e., change the terms) of her Trust or even terminate (i.e., revoke) the Trust altogether and have the Trust property placed back into her own name. If she does not revoke her Trust during her lifetime, once she dies the Trust becomes irrevocable, and her Successor Trustee must follow the terms of the Trust Agreement as written. If the Trust says to give the Trust property to certain beneficiaries, the Successor Trustee will do so, and without the need for Probate. If the Trust directs the Successor Trustee to hold property in Trust and use the money to take care of a member of Elaine's family, in the manner described in the Trust Agreement, the Successor Trustee will do so.

Setting up a Trust has many good features.

☆☆ AVOID PROBATE

In Ohio, Probate can be time consuming and very expensive. Both the Personal Representative and his attorney are entitled to payment for their services. These fees can be significant. It may be necessary to employ accountants and appraisers, and real estate brokers to sell property as well. If you have property in two states, then two Probate procedures may be necessary (one in each state) and that could be costly in time, effort and money. If the Trust is properly drafted and your property placed into the Trust, you should be able to avoid Probate altogether.

☆ FEDERAL ESTATE TAX SAVINGS

Many people think that the federal Estate Tax will be phased out so that by 2010, no Estate Taxes will be due regardless of the size of an Estate. But under current law in 2011, the Estate Tax is scheduled to be reinstated and those who own property worth more than $1,000,000 will once again be subject to a sizeable Estate Tax. A couple with an Estate in excess of a million dollars can reduce the risk of an Estate Tax by setting up a Trust, so that each partner can take advantage of his own Estate Tax Exclusion.

For example, if a couple's assets total two million dollars, they can set up a Trust that separates the money into two Trusts once one partner dies. The Trust can be arranged so that the surviving spouse is free to use the income from both Trusts. Once both partners are deceased, the beneficiaries of their respective Trusts will inherit the funds, hopefully with no Estate Tax due. If the couple does not set up a Trust and continues to hold all of their property jointly, the last to die will own the two million dollars with only one Estate Tax Exclusion available — with one million dollars subject to Estate Taxes.

☆ CARE FOR FAMILY MEMBER:
You can make provision in your Trust to care for a
minor child or family member after you die. If your beneficiary is a minor, you can direct your Successor Trustee to
distribute the child's inheritance at different times. For
example, you can direct your Successor Trustee to give the
beneficiary a certain amount of money when he is 18, then
21, then 25, then 30, etc.

If your intended beneficiary has a creditor problem,
you can set up a *Spendthrift Trust* to protect the Trust
funds from the claims of creditors. You can direct your
Successor Trustee to spend Trust funds for you beneficiary's
health care, education, and living expenses, and nothing
more. With a properly drafted Spendthrift provision the
Trust funds cannot be reached by the creditors of the
beneficiary. Of course, once Trust funds are distributed to
the beneficiary, his creditors have the right to demand
payment from those monies (*Domo v. McCarthy*, 612 N.E.2d
706, (Ohio, 1993)).

NO CREDITOR PROTECTION FOR SETTLOR
You can set up a Spendthrift Trust for a beneficiary, but
not for yourself. Because property held in your Revocable
Living Trust is freely accessible to you, it is likewise
accessible to your creditors both before and after your
death. If you die owing money, your creditors can have a
Personal Representative appointed to locate funds to pay
those debts. The Personal Representative can require that
your Trust property be used to pay for those debts
(ORC 5815.22).

☆ PRIVACY

Your Living Trust is a private document. No one but your Successor Trustee and your beneficiaries need ever read it. If you leave property in a Will and there is a Probate procedure, the Will must be filed with the court, where it becomes a public document. Anyone can go to the courthouse, read your Will and see who you did (or did not) provide for in your Will. Records in the Probate Court (inventories, creditor's claims, etc.) are open to public scrutiny. In many states, court records are now available on the Internet!

LEASE SAFE DEPOSIT BOX AS TRUSTEE

One of the benefits of having a Living Trust is that you can lease the safe deposit box in your name as Trustee. When you lease the safe deposit box you can have an agreement with the bank giving your Successor Trustee free access to the safe deposit box in the event of your incapacity or death.

This protects your privacy. As explained in Chapter 3, if you hold the safe deposit box in your name only, access to the box is restricted upon your death. No one can take possession of the contents of your box without a Court order, but your next of kin can ask the bank to be allowed to examine the contents of the box to see if your Will is there.

By leasing a safe deposit box as Trustee, only you and your Successor Trustee need ever know of the contents of the box.

☆☆ AVOID APPOINTMENT OF A GUARDIAN

Once you have a Trust you do not need to worry about who will take care of property you place in the Trust. Should you become disabled, or too aged to handle your finances, your Successor Trustee will take over the care of your Trust property. If you do not make provision for the care of your property, it may be necessary for a Court to appoint a Guardian of your property. Guardianship is a good thing to avoid, not only because of the cost of the procedure, but also to avoid the embarrassment of a Court coming to the conclusion that you are not competent to manage your own finances.

Before appointing a Guardian, the Court will conduct a hearing to determine whether you are competent to manage your property. You are entitled to have your own attorney at the hearing. If you do not have an attorney the Court can appoint one for you (ORC 2111.031) If the Court determines that you do not have the capacity to handle your finances, he will appoint a Guardian. The Court may order the Guardian to obtain a bond for the protection of your property (ORC 2109.04). Once appointed, the Guardian will take possession of your property and file an inventory with the Court. He will manage your property and at least once every two years report to the Court for monies spent (ORC 2109.302). The Guardian may need to employ an accountant to assist with these reports. He needs to employ an attorney to establish the Guardianship and then see that it is properly administered. The Guardian, and his attorney are entitled to be paid for their efforts on your behalf.

Court filing fees, the cost of a bond, accounting fees, Guardian's fees, your attorney fees, the Guardian's attorney fees, are all charged to your Estate (that's your money!). And these expenses goes on year after year until you are restored to capacity or die.

THE PROBLEMS

With all these perks, you may be ready to call your attorney to make an appointment to set up a Trust, but before doing so there are a few things you need to consider:

☒ COMPLEXITY

A Trust is a fairly complex document, often 30 pages long. It needs to be that long because you are establishing a vehicle to take care of your property during your lifetime, as well as after your death. The Trust usually is written in "legalese," so it may take you considerable time and effort to understand it. It is important to have your Trust document prepared by an attorney who has the patience to work with you until you fully understand each paragraph of the document and are satisfied that what it says is what you really want.

☒ COST

Because of the thoroughness of the document and the fact that it is custom designed for you, a Trust will cost much more to draft than a simple Will. In addition to the initial cost of the Trust, it can be expensive to maintain the Trust should you become disabled or die. Your Successor Trustee has the right to charge for his duties as Trustee, as well as to charge for any specialized services performed. A financial institution can charge to serve as Successor Trustee, and also charge to manage the Trust portfolio. If you decide to have a financial institution serve as Trustee, then it is important that you compare the fee schedules of different institutions.

You can choose an attorney, or an accountant, or a financial planner, to serve as Trustee, but this may create a conflict of interest because the professional can use his position as Trustee to generate fees.

If you decide to appoint a professional as Trustee you should have a fee agreement stating what will be charged for his duties as Trustee and what will be charged for professional work done on behalf of the Trust. The fee agreement should be included in the Trust document with a provision that whoever accepts the job of Successor Trustee, agrees to accept the fee as provided in the Trust document.

You may decide to appoint your spouse or a family member as Successor Trustee, who may want little, or no, compensation. Regardless of who you choose to be Successor Trustee, you need to come to a fee agreement. The agreement can be for a set amount or a percentage of the value of the Trust, or other method to be used to determine his compensation.

☒ YOU MAY NEED YOUR SPOUSE'S PERMISSION TO TRANSFER PROPERTY INTO YOUR TRUST

Most married couples prepare a Trust as part of their overall Estate Plan. Sometimes a married person has a Trust that was prepared prior to the marriage, or he may decide to create a Trust to care for children from a previous marriage. In such case, it may be necessary to have the spouse agree, in writing, to the transfer of real property into the Trust. Under Ohio law, a spouse has a Dower right to a one-third Life Estate interest in property you own during your married life. If you place real property into your Trust without permission from your spouse, (s)he can assert those rights before or after your death.

You do not need your spouse's permission to transfer personal property into the trust (bank accounts, securities, insurance policies, etc.) Your spouse will not have any right to personal property you place into the Trust unless you make provision for your spouse in the Trust document (ORC 2103.02, 2106.01(D)).

⊠ PROBATE MIGHT STILL BE NECESSARY

The Trust only works for those items that you place in the Trust. If you own property in your name only, then upon your death, a Probate procedure might be necessary in order to transfer the property to your beneficiary. For example, if you purchase a security in your name only, without a "Transfer On Death" designation to a named beneficiary or to your Trust, then a Probate procedure may be necessary to determine who should inherit the security.

The attorney who prepares the Trust usually creates a safety net for such situations. He prepares a Will for you to sign at the same time you sign the Trust. The Will makes your Trust the beneficiary of your Probate Estate. If you own anything in your name only and a Probate procedure is necessary, the Will directs your Personal Representative to make that asset part of your Trust by transferring the asset to your Successor Trustee. Your Successor Trustee will add that asset to your Trust (ORC 2107.63).

The Will prepared by the attorney is called a *Pour Over Will* because it is designed to "pour" any asset titled in your name only, into the Trust. Having the Will ensures that all of your property will go to the beneficiaries named in your Trust. But the downside of holding property in your name only is that a full Probate procedure may be necessary just to get that asset into your Trust. If avoiding Probate is your goal, holding property in your name only, defeats that goal.

You can ensure that a Probate procedure will not be necessary by transferring your assets into your Trust during your lifetime, but if you neglect to put something into your Trust, the Pour Over Will stands by to transfer that asset into your Trust.

⊠ TAXES MAY STILL BE A PROBLEM

While you are operating the Trust as Trustee, all of the property held in your Revocable Living Trust is taxed as if you were holding that property in your own name. If the value of your Trust property exceeds the Estate Tax Exclusion value, taxes will be due once you die. If all you own is held in your Trust, your Successor Trustee will need to pay those taxes from the Trust property.

Those who have Estates large enough to incur Estate Taxes also need to think about how taxes will be paid on other taxable transfers. For example, suppose you and your brother bought a home as Joint Tenants With Right of Survivorship. If you each contributed equally to the purchase, and the property is now worth one million dollars, your brother will inherit your half million dollar share. If you also own two million dollars in other property, all of which is in your Trust, your Taxable Estate is $2,500,000.

Unless your Trust directs otherwise, each beneficiary of your Estate is responsible to pay a proportionate share of the Estate Taxes. If federal Estate Taxes are reinstated so that anything over one million dollars is taxable at a rate of 40%, your Estate Tax will be $600,000. Your brother will need to contribute his prorated share of the Estate Taxes:
$$\$500,000/\$2,500,000 = .2$$
$$20\% \text{ of } \$600,000 = \$120,000.$$

But suppose your brother doesn't have that kind of cash? Should he be forced to sell his home in order to pay the taxes? Should your Successor Trustee use your Trust property to pay your brother's taxes with a promise that he will reimburse the beneficiaries of your Trust at a later date? An experienced Estate Planning attorney can suggest any number of ways to head off such problems.

⊠ ☆ THE TRUST IS LEGALLY ENFORCEABLE

Your Successor Trustee will take over the administration of your Trust upon your incapacity or death. Should there be a dispute regarding the administration of the Trust, your beneficiary (or your Successor Trustee) can petition the Court to settle the matter. For example, your Successor Trustee is entitled to reasonable compensation. If you did not set the amount he is to be paid in the Trust Agreement and the beneficiaries object to the amount he is charging, they can ask the Court to determine his compensation (ORC 2101.24).

We gave this section a cross and a star because the right to have a Trust enforced or administered by the Court is a double edged sword. It is great to have the Court protect the rights of your beneficiaries, but the cost of a court battle could be greater than if your Estate was Probated and the money simply distributed to your beneficiaries.

The beneficiaries of your Trust are at a financial disadvantage in a dispute with your Successor Trustee. The Court can require your Trustee to be personally liable for his legal costs, but that only happens if the Trustee acted illegally or unreasonably. In most cases, the Trustee will be able to charge the expense of defending his actions to your Trust and your beneficiaries will pay for their legal expenses out of their own pockets.

Win or lose, there will be just that much less for your beneficiaries to inherit.

Although all of the methods discussed in this Chapter can be used to transfer property without the need for Probate, each method may have a downside that is objectionable to you. Maybe you don't have enough money to warrant the cost of setting up the Trust at this time. Holding property jointly with another may raise issues of security and independence. Holding property so that it goes directly to a few beneficiaries in a Pay On Death account may not be as flexible as you wish. This may be the case if you wish to give gifts to several charities or to minor children instead of just one or two beneficiaries.

For example, if you hold all your property so that it goes to your son without the need for Probate, and you ask him to use some of the money for your grandchild's education, it may be that your grandchild gets none of the money because your son is sued or falls upon hard times. If you keep your property in your name only and leave a Will giving a certain amount of money for your grandchild, the child will know exactly how much money you left and the purpose of that gift.

After taking into account all the pros and cons of avoiding Probate, you may well opt for a Will and a Probate procedure. If you make such a decision, it is important to keep in mind that Estate Planning is not an "all or nothing" choice. You can arrange your Estate so that certain items pass automatically to your intended beneficiary, and other items can be left in your name only, to be distributed as part of a Probate procedure. By arranging your finances in this manner, you can reduce the value of your Probate Estate, and that in turn should reduce the cost of Probate.

Your Ohio Will

Many people decide that the Will is the best route to go but do not act upon it, thinking it unnecessary to prepare a Will until they are very old and about to die. But according to reports published by the National Center for Health Statistics (a division of the U.S. Department of Health and Human Services) 2 of every 10 people who die in any given year are under the age of 60.

Twenty percent may seem like a small number until it hits close to home as it did with a young couple. They were having difficulty conceiving a child. They went from doctor to doctor until they met someone just beginning his practice. With his knowledge of the latest advances in medicine, he was able to help them.

The birth of their child was a moment of joy and gratitude. They asked a nurse to take a picture of them all together — the proud parents, the newborn child and the doctor who made it all possible. Happiness radiated from the picture, but within 6 months, one of them would be dead.

You might think it was the child. An infant's life is so fragile. SIDS and all manner of childhood diseases can threaten a little one. But no, he grew up a healthy young man.

If you looked at the picture, you might guess the husband. Overweight and stressed out; his ruddy complexion suggested high blood pressure. He looked like a typical heart- attack-prone Type A personality.

No, he was fine and went on to enjoy raising his son.

Probably it was the wife. She had such a difficult time with the pregnancy and the delivery was especially hard. Maybe it was all too much for her.

No, she recovered and later had two more children.

It was the doctor who was killed in a collision with a truck.

WHY A WILL IS NECESSARY

Though we all agree that one never knows, still people put off making a Will figuring that if they die before getting around to it, Ohio law will take over and their property will be distributed in the manner that they would have wanted anyway. The problem with that logic is the complexity of Ohio's Laws of Descent. If you are survived by a spouse, child, parent or sibling, it isn't too difficult to figure out who will inherit your property. But if none of these survive you, the ultimate beneficiary of your property may not be the person you would have chosen, had you taken the time to make a Will.

Others think that it is not necessary to have a Will because they arranged their finances so that all of their property will be inherited without the need for Probate. But money could come into your Estate after your death. This could happen in any number of ways. You might die in a house fire, or a flood. Your insurance company may need to pay for damages done to your home. You might be killed in a car accident caused by the wrongful act of someone. In such case, a Personal Representative may need to be appointed to sue on behalf of your Estate.

As explained in Chapter 6, without a Will, the Court will use an order of priority as set by Ohio law to appoint a Personal Representative. The person chosen by the Court may not be the person you would have chosen to settle your Estate. And as we will see in this Chapter, there are other important reasons to make a Will.

 SET THE PERSONAL REPRESENTATIVE'S FEE

An important reason to make a Will is to choose your Personal Representative and to come to an understanding about how much compensation he will receive. You can state that value in your Will.

 THE PERSONAL REPRESENTATIVE
CAN SEEK MORE MONEY

You can put the amount of agreed compensation in your Will; however your Personal Representative can reject that amount and ask for the amount allowed under law (ORC 2113.36). See Page 172 for those values. To avoid the problem, you can have your attorney draft an agreement that you and your Personal Representative sign and incorporate into your Will (ORC 2107.05).

Having a separate fee agreement will not stop your Personal Representative from asking for more money, but with such an agreement, the Court will not agree to the increase unless something unusual occurs (such as a law suit) causing much more work than the ordinary Probate procedure.

You also need to keep in mind that the Personal Representative's fee is just to administer the Estate. It does not include payment for professional work he may do while settling the Estate. For example, if you appoint your attorney as Personal Representative, he can agree to the amount stated in the Will for his role as Personal Representative, and then ask the Court to award him attorney's fees as well.

The same goes for any other professional. If you appoint your accountant to serve as Personal Representative, he is entitled to receive compensation for his work as Personal Representative and also for any accounting work he does such as preparing and filing tax returns; preparing an inventory and doing an accounting for the beneficiaries. A financial planner who serves as Personal Representative may be compensated for his management of the Estate property (buying and selling securities, taking care of rental property, etc.) in addition to his fee to administer the Estate.

But the main problem with appointing a professional as your Personal Representative is the same as appointing a professional to serve as the Successor Trustee of your Trust; namely, that it creates a potential conflict of interest. The professional can use his position as Personal Representative to generate fees that may not have been necessary if someone else settled the Estate.

When choosing a Personal Representative, consider the relationship of the Personal Representative to the beneficiaries and determine whether it would be better to appoint a non-professional for the job.

MAKE GIFTS OF YOUR PERSONAL PROPERTY
Another benefit to making a Will is that you can make provision for who will get your personal property, including your car. If you make a gift of your car in your Will, then it will be relatively simple for your car to be transferred to the beneficiary. If you do not make a specific gift of your car, it is available for your surviving spouse to take as described in Chapter 4. The same applies to any motor boat you may own.

If your surviving spouse does not want your car or boat, or if you are single, it will be up to your Personal Representative to decide what to do with the car. He can sell it and include the proceeds of the sale in the Estate funds to be distributed to your residuary beneficiaries; or he can give the car to one beneficiary of your Estate as part of that beneficiary's share of the Estate.

SMALL GIFTS MATTER

Many who have lost someone close to them report that the distribution of small personal items caused the greatest conflict. If you arrange your finances so that no Probate procedure is necessary, your next of kin will need to decide how to distribute your personal effects. Without guidance from you and no Personal Representative with authority to make decisions, there could be disagreement and hard feelings, over items of little monetary value. If you make a Will, you can include a list of gifts of personal effects in your Will and your Personal Representative will distribute the gifts according to your directions. You can have a separate list of gifts of personal property, provided you refer to that list in your Will (ORC 2107.05). You can change the separate list, but you need to sign and date changes made to that list.

Of course, you cannot list each and every item you own, but you can instruct your Personal Representative to allow certain family members to take their choice of items not mentioned in your Will. If two or more family members want the same item, have your Personal Representative use an appropriate lottery system (coin toss, high card in a cut of a deck of cards, etc.) to decide who "wins."

🗐 MAKE ADJUSTMENT FOR PRIOR GIFTS

You can use your Will to make adjustments for gifts or loans given during your lifetime. For example, if you loaned money to a family member and do not expect to be repaid, you can deduct the loan from that person's inheritance. Of course, it may be that you are not concerned with inequities. That was the case of an aged woman who had three children, Paul, Rita and Frank, her youngest. Frank always seemed to need some assistance from his mother. She often "loaned" him money he never repaid.

Her other children were responsible and independent. Paul was married and had children of his own. He decided to purchase a house but was having trouble accumulating the down payment. His mother agreed to lend him the money. Paul and his wife offered to give his mother a mortgage on the property. The mother said a simple promissory note from Paul was sufficient, and she would have her attorney draft the note.

The attorney drafted the note but was concerned about the inequity "You never made a Will. Were you to die, each of your children will inherit an equal amount of money. If Paul still owes money on this promissory note, he will either need to pay the balance to your Estate, or have it subtracted from the amount he inherits (ORC 2113.59). All of the money you gave to Frank will not count towards his inheritance unless you make it clear that you considered the money you gave to Frank to be an advancement of his inheritance. You can do this by making an adjustment in a Will, or by having Frank give you a promissory note for any outstanding debt.

"It's O.K." replied the mother "I love all my children equally . . . some are a little more equal than others."

⬛ MAKE PROVISION FOR PAYMENT OF DEBTS AND TAXES

If monies are owed on your car, home or other property, the beneficiaries of that item will inherit the loan along with the gift (ORC 2113.52). Taxes are another concern for those Estates large enough to be subject to Estate Taxes. Federal law require that Estate Taxes be paid by the beneficiaries of the Estate in proportion to the value received, unless the decedent made some other arrangements to pay for the taxes. If you make no provision for the payment of taxes, whoever inherits your property will pay a percentage of the taxes based on the amount they receive (26 U.S.C. 6324 (a)(2)).

If this is not as you wish, you can direct your Personal Representative to pay all of your debts and taxes from your Probate Estate. If you do so, those who inherit property from a non-Probate transfer will not contribute to the payment of your debts and taxes. All of the money you owe will be paid from your Probate Estate. This means that the amount your residuary beneficiaries receive will be reduced by the amount paid for debts and taxes.

⬛ CHOOSE A GUARDIAN FOR YOUR CHILD

Each parent has the right to name someone to be Guardian of their minor child in the event that the parent dies before the child is grown, and the other parent is deceased or incapacitated. You can do this as part of your Will, or in a separate writing that is signed in the presence of two witnesses and a notary public (ORC 2111.121).

The person you name to be Guardian can assume the care of the child upon your death, but that person needs to be appointed as the child's legal Guardian by the Probate court.

It is important to name someone compatible with the child. If not, and the child is over the age of 14, the child has the right to express his choice of Guardian. The judge will give the preference to the person you choose as Guardian of the property of the child (i.e., money you leave to the child). But he will give preference to the person chosen by the child to serve as Guardian of his person (i.e., his custodial Guardian).

In all cases, the judge has final say as to who will serve as Guardian. He will be guided by the best interests of the child. If the judge determines that person you, or your child chooses as Guardian, is not qualified to be Guardian, he will appoint someone else for the job (ORC 2111.12).

MAKE PROVISION TO CONTINUE FAMILY BUSINESS
If you are the sole proprietor of a business, you need to give considerable thought to what will happen to that business in the event of your incapacity or death. Can the business continue to operate without you? Is it your intent that whoever inherits your business take over its daily operations or do you think it best to have the business sold and the proceeds of the sale given to your beneficiary?

Under Ohio law, the Personal Representative can continue the operation of the business for up to four months, without permission from the Court. After that he will need Court permission to continue to operate the business. Generally, the Court sets a hearing on the matter giving the surviving spouse and beneficiaries of the Estate an opportunity to raise any objection they may have (ORC 2113.30). All this legal hassle and expense can be avoided if you make specific provision in your Will for the operation and transfer of your business.

AVOIDING A CHALLENGE TO YOUR WILL

Some people think that preparing a Will is a simple thing — something they can do themselves. But writing a Will is like figure skating. It is harder than it looks. A Will needs to be clearly worded. A sentence that can be read in two different ways can lead to a dispute over what you intended; and that could result in a long and expensive Court battle. Your Will needs to be properly witnessed and signed. If not, it could be challenged on that basis (ORC 2107.03).

If the challenge is successful, the Court may refuse to admit the Will to Probate, and your property will be distributed according to the Ohio Laws of Descent and Distribution.

If you are serious about having your property distributed exactly as you wish, it is best to have the document prepared by an attorney who is experienced in Estate Planning. Should there be a challenge to your Will, he will be able to testify that the Will was prepared according to your specific instructions and that you knew exactly what you were doing and were fully competent when you signed it.

Having your Will prepared by an experienced Estate Planning attorney may make it difficult for someone to successfully challenge your Will, but it won't stop them from at least trying. As discussed in Chapter 5, there are any number of reasons to challenge a Will. If you are concerned that someone will challenge the way you have decided to distribute your property, there are several preventative measures you can take.

NO GIFT TO ATTORNEY

Ohio courts have presumed that undue influence occurs whenever an attorney, who is unrelated to the Will maker, is named as a beneficiary under a Will prepared by that attorney (*Krischbaum v. Dillon*, 567 N.E.2d 1291 (Ohio, 1991)). If you wish to make a gift to your attorney — even if that attorney is related to you through blood or marriage, it is best to have some other, independent, attorney prepare your Will.

NO CONTEST CLAUSE

You can have your attorney include a **no contest** provision in your Will stating that if a beneficiary named in your Will challenges any provision in the Will, he will inherit none of your Probate Estate. Such a provision is called an **In Terrorem Clause** because it is designed to cause fear (if not terror) in the heart of your beneficiary. Many states will not enforce such a clause, because they want people to have the right to challenge a Will, and let the Court decide whether that challenge is proper. Ohio does not have a law either condoning or prohibiting a no contest provision. However, Ohio Courts have indicated a willingness to uphold an In Terrorem Clause, depending on the given circumstances (*Kirkbride v. Hickok*, 98 N.E.2d 815 (Ohio, 1951)).

MAKE PROVISION FOR YOUR SPOUSE

Your surviving spouse has the right to inherit at least as much from your Probate Estate as if you died without a Will (See Chapter 5 for that amount). If you leave less than your spouse would have received under Ohio's Laws of Descent, (s)he has up to five months to challenge the amount given in your Will, and ask the Court to be given as much as allowed under the Laws of Descent. (ORC 2106.01).

REVOCABLE LIVING TRUST

If you place all of your property into a Trust, upon your death it will be transferred to your beneficiaries without going through Probate. This avoids the need for your Will to be Probated (i.e., proved). As explained in Chapter 7, your surviving spouse has Dower rights in real property you own, but not in your personal property. If you place all of your personal property into your Trust, under current law, your spouse will not be able to challenge the way your personal property is distributed.

However, laws change. In most states, a surviving spouse has the right to demand an Elective Share of property regardless of whether that property was placed in Trust.

HAVE COURT DECLARE WILL TO BE VALID

In Ohio, you can ask the Probate Court in the county of your residence for a Declaratory Judgment stating that your Will is valid. To do so, you will need to name all of the beneficiaries of your Will and all those people who would inherit your property if you die without a Will, as defendants (ORC 2107.081). This could be an expensive way to go if one or more of your relatives decide to argue the point.

If the Court declares your Will to be valid, there is still the problem of what happens to the Will if you decide to modify or revoke it. You are free to revoke or modify your Will at any time, but your new Will or a *codicil* (change to the old Will) does not have the protection as the Will covered by the Declaratory Judgment. To continue protection, you will need to go through the Declaratory Judgment procedure all over again.

STORING YOUR WILL

Once you sign your Will, you may wonder where to store it. Your attorney may suggest that he place it in his vault for safekeeping. By doing so, he ensures that your heirs will need to contact him as soon as you die. This does not mean that they are required to employ him should a Probate proceeding be necessary. It only means that he will have an opportunity for future employment.

But there are problems with such an arrangement. The Will could be lost or mistaken for another Will of a client who might happen to have the same name. That happened in at least one case. The attorney prepared Wills for two people with the same name and similar family circumstances. When one person died the attorney submitted the wrong Will to Probate.

Luckily the error was quickly discovered. The decedent had a distinctive signature. The family challenged the validity of the Will based on the unfamiliar signature and the way the property was to be distributed. They knew the decedent would never have distributed his property in the manner stated in the Will.

If you decide to allow your attorney to store the Will, you need assurance that the attorney will be responsible for the document.

You should get a receipt and something in writing that says:

⇨ The attorney accepts full responsibility for the storage of the Will. Should it be lost or damaged, he will redraft the document for you to sign, and at no cost to you. If you are deceased, he will, at no cost to your heirs, present sufficient evidence to the Court to accept a valid copy of the Will into Probate.

⇨ There will be no charge to you, or your heirs, for the storage and retrieval of the document.

⇨ Should he sell his practice, retire, or die, he or the successor to his practice, will return the original document to you.

STORE IN SAFE DEPOSIT BOX

You might consider placing your Will in a safe deposit box that you lease at a bank. The only problem with the bank safe deposit box is convenient access. As we explained in Chapter 3, If you hold a safe deposit box in your name only, should you die, the bank will restrict access to the safe deposit box. For those who are happily married, the solution to the problem of accessing the safe deposit box after death, may be to lease the box jointly with your spouse such that each of you has free access to the box.

However, this may not be the best choice if you think your spouse will be unhappy with certain provisions made in your Will. Some Wills never see the light of day for this reason. It may be better to keep the safe deposit box in your name only. The bank may allow family members to inspect your safe deposit box, under the supervision of an officer or employee of the company. The bank will allow your Will to be removed after making a copy of the document (ORC 5731.39).

As explained in Chapter 7, those who have a Trust can solve the problem by giving their Successor Trustee joint access to the safe deposit box. If you are single and do not have a Trust, you can lease the box jointly with a trusted family member. Of course, if privacy and security are important to you, this might offset any concern for the convenience of your beneficiaries. In such case, consider keeping the document in a fireproof safe deposit box within your home. You can give a duplicate key to the person you chose to be your Personal Representative.

STORE IT WITH COURT

Perhaps the best solution is to store your Will with the Probate Court in the county of your residence. The cost is nominal and you are free to retrieve the Will from the Court in the event that you move or decide to change your Will (ORC 2107.07).

Regardless of where you choose to store your Will, let your Personal Representative know that you have a Will and how to retrieve it in the event of your death.

CHOOSING THE RIGHT ESTATE PLAN

Joint Ownership?
A Pay On Death bank account?
A Transfer On Death Security?
A Will?
A Trust?
A Life Insurance Policy???

Chapters 7 and 8 offer so many options that the reader may be more confused than when he was blissfully unenlightened.

As with most things in life, you may find there are no ultimate solutions, just alternatives. The right choice for you is the one that best accomplishes your goal. This being the case, you first need to determine what you want to accomplish with the money you leave. Think about what will happen to your property if you were to die suddenly, without making any plan different from the one you now have.

> Who will be responsible to pay your bills?
> Who will inherit your property?
> Will Probate be necessary?

If the answers to these questions are not as you wish, you need to work to arrange your property to accomplish your goals.

For those with significant assets — especially those with Estates large enough to pay Estate Taxes, and for many others with special circumstances, e.g., blended families, or those with disabled family members, a trip to an experienced Estate Planning attorney may be well worth the consultation fee.

Your Estate Plan Record 9

Once you are satisfied with your Estate Plan, the final thing to consider is whether your heirs will be able to locate your assets once you are gone.

Most people have their business records in one place, their Will in another place, car titles and deeds in still another place. When someone dies, their beneficiaries may feel as if they are playing a game of "hide and seek" with the decedent. The game might be fun were it not for the fact that an unlocated item may be forever lost. For example, suppose you die in an accident and no one knows you are insured by your credit card company for accidental death in the amount of $25,000. The only one to profit is the insurance company, which is just that much richer because no one told them that you died as a result of an accident.

And how about a key to a safe deposit box located in another state? Will anyone find it? Even if they find the key, how will they find the box?

It is not difficult to arrange things so that your affairs are always in order. It amounts to being aware of what you own (and owe) and keeping a record of your possessions. A side benefit is that by doing so, you will always know where all your business records are. If you ever spent time trying to collect information to file your taxes or trying to find a lost stock or bond certificate, you will appreciate the value of organizing your records.

ORGANIZING YOUR RECORDS

Heirs need all the help they can get. It is difficult enough dealing with the loss, without the frustration of trying to locate important documents. Your heirs will have no problem locating your assets if you keep all of your records in a single place. It can be a desk drawer or a file cabinet or even a shoe box. It is helpful if you keep a separate file or folder for each type of investment. You might consider setting up the following folders:

🗁 THE BANK & SECURITIES FOLDER

Store your original certificates for stocks, bonds, mutual funds, and certificates of deposit in a folder labeled **BANK & SECURITIES**. In addition to the original certificate, include a copy of the contract you signed with each financial institution. The contract will show where you have funds and who you named as beneficiary or joint owner of the account. If someone owes you money and signed a promissory note or mortgage identifying you as the lender, store these documents in this folder as well.

If you have a safe deposit box, keep a record of its location and the number of the box. Keep a copy of all of the items stored in the box in this folder. If you have an extra key to the box, put it here.

E-bank Accounts If you are doing your banking on-line, it is important to keep a record of your passwords so that your family can access the account in the event of your incapacity or death. The same applies if you have on-line brokerage or installment loan accounts. Keep a paper record of these accounts in this folder.

🗂 THE INSURANCE FOLDER

The INSURANCE FOLDER is for each insurance policy that you own, be it life insurance, car insurance, homeowner's insurance or a health care insurance policy. If you purchased real property, you probably received a title commitment at closing and the title insurance policy some weeks later when you received your original deed from recording. If you cannot locate the title insurance policy, contact the closing agent and have him send you a copy of your title policy.

🗂 THE PENSION AND ANNUITY FOLDER

If you have a pension or annuity, put all of the documents relating to the pension in this folder. Include the telephone number and/or address of the person to contact in the event of your death.

FOR FEDERAL RETIREES If you are a federal retiree, you should have received your PERSONAL IDENTIFICATION NUMBER (PIN). The person who will inherit your pension (your *survivor annuitant*) should have his own PIN as well. It is relatively simple to obtain your survivor's PIN during your lifetime, but it may be difficult and/or stressful for your survivor annuitant to work through the system once you are gone.

Survivor annuitant benefits are not automatic. Your survivor annuitant must apply for them by submitting a death claim to the Office of Personnel Management. Your survivor needs to know that it is necessary to apply and also how to apply. You can get printed information about how to apply for benefits from the Office Of Personnel Management (see Page 34). Keep the printed information in this file.

📁　　THE DEED FOLDER

Many people save every scrap of paper associated with the closing of real property. If you closed recently on real estate and there was a mortgage involved in the purchase, you probably walked away from closing with enough paper to wallpaper your kitchen. If you wish, you can keep all of those papers in a separate file that identifies the property, for example:

CLOSING PAPERS FOR THE SANDUSKY PROPERTY

Place the original deed (or a copy if the original is in a safe deposit box) in a separate DEED FOLDER. Include cemetery deeds, condominium deeds, cooperative shares to real property, timesharing certificates, deed to out of state property, etc. Also include a copy of related documents such as an Abstract of Title, or a recorded Condominium Approval. If you have a title insurance policy, put the original in the insurance folder, and a copy in this folder. If you have a mortgage on your property, put a copy of the recorded mortgage and promissory note in a separate LIABILITY FOLDER.

LOCATING REAL PROPERTY

If you own a vacant lot, your beneficiaries will find the deed (or a copy) in this folder but that deed will not contain the address of that property because it doesn't have one. The post office does not assign a street address until there is a building on the site. Your beneficiaries can get the location of the property from city or county records. But why make things hard for them? Include a handwritten note in this folder that tells them exactly how to locate the property.

🗁 THE LIABILITY FOLDER

The LIABILITY FOLDER should contain all loan documents of debts that you owe. For example, if you purchased real property and have a mortgage on that property, put a copy of the mortgage and promissory note in this folder. If you owe money on a car, put the loan documents in this folder. If you have a credit card, put a copy of the contract you signed with the credit card company in this folder. A lease is a liability, because you contracted to pay a certain amount for the period of the lease, so include a copy of any lease agreement in this folder.

If you have a mortgage on your property, put a copy of the recorded mortgage and promissory note in this folder. Once the mortgage is paid off, the lender must have a *Satisfaction of Mortgage* recorded within 90 days of the final payment. The Satisfaction needs to be recorded in the county where the property is located. Ohio law requires that the borrower pay for the recording of the satisfaction (ORC 5301.36).

Keep the recorded Satisfaction together with the deed to the property. Remember to remove the paid mortgage from your Liability Folder.

Many people never take the time to calculate their *net worth* (what a person owns less what he owes). By having a record of your assets and outstanding debts, you can calculate your net worth whenever you wish.

📁 THE PERSONAL PROPERTY FOLDER

MOTOR VEHICLES

Put all motor vehicle titles in a Personal Property folder. This includes cars, mobile homes, boats, planes, etc. If you owe money on the vehicle, the lender may have possession of the title certificate. If such is the case, put a copy of the title certificate and registration in this folder and a copy of the loan documents in a separate liability folder.

If you own a boat or plane, identify the location of the motor vehicle. For example, if you are leasing space in an airplane hangar or in a marina, keep a copy of the leasing agreement in this file.

JEWELRY

If you own expensive jewelry, keep a picture of the item together with the sales receipt or written appraisal in this folder.

COLLECTOR'S ITEMS

If you own a valuable art or coin collection, or any other item of significant value, include a picture of the item in this file. Also include evidence of ownership of the item, such as a sales receipt or a certificate of authenticity, or a written appraisal of the property.

🗂 THE PERSONAL RECORDS FOLDER

The **PERSONAL RECORDS FOLDER** should include documents that relate to you personally, such as a birth certificate, naturalization papers, marriage certificate, divorce papers, military records, Social Security card, etc. If you have a Power of Attorney for finances or a Durable Power of Attorney For Health Care, or a Living Will, you can place these document in this folder, or in your Estate Planning folder. If you placed the original document in a safe deposit box, keep a copy in this folder together with the location of the original.

🗂 THE ESTATE PLANNING DOCUMENT FOLDER

Place your Estate Planning documents (Will, Trust, Antenuptial Agreement, burial, funeral arrangements, etc.) in a separate folder. If your attorney has your original documents, or you placed the original in a safe deposit box, place a copy of the document in this folder together with instructions about how to find the original. If you deposited your Will with the Court you should have a Certificate of Deposit (ORC 2107.07). Store the Certificate in this folder.

Regardless of where you store your Will or Trust, it is important to keep a copy of the document in your home. Over the years you may forget what provision you made. Keeping a copy in your home may save you a trip to the safe deposit box to determine whether you need to update the document.

📁 THE TAX RECORD FOLDER

Your Personal Representative (or next of kin) will need to file your final income tax returns. Keep a copy of your tax returns (both federal and state) for the past three years in your Tax Record Folder.

As explained in Chapter 2, beginning in 2010, there will be a cap on the step-up basis to 4.3 million dollars for property inherited by the spouse and 1.3 million dollars for property inherited by anyone else. It is important to keep a record of the basis of your property, not only for your heirs, but for yourself should you decide to sell the property during your lifetime. If you purchase real property, you need to keep a record of the purchase price as well as monies you paid to improve the property. For condominium units, that will include special assessments for improvements to the property.

You will need these records to determine whether there will be a Capital Gains Tax on the transfer. Your accountant can help you set up a bookkeeping system to keep a running record of your basis in everything you own of value.

STORING YOUR FILES

The information stored in your files is important and may be difficult, if not impossible, to replace. Consider investing in a fire proof safe large enough to accommodate your files. Give a duplicate key to the safe to whomever you appointed as Personal Representative or Executor of your Estate.

THE *If I Die* FILE

Many do not have the time, nor inclination, to "play" with all these folders. They do not anticipate an immediate demise. Getting hit by a truck, or dying in a fiery plane crash is not something to think about, much less prepare for. But consider that death is not the only problem. You could take suddenly ill (say with a stroke) and become incapacitated. Even the most time-starved optimist should have a murmur of concern that his loved ones will be left with a mess should something unforeseen happen.

If you do not feel like doing a complete job of organizing your records at this time, consider an abridged version. You can set up a single file with a list of all you own and the location of each item. You need to make that file easily accessible to whomever you wish to manage your affairs in the event of your incapacity or death. You can do this by letting that person know of the existence of the file and how to get it in an emergency; or keeping the file in an easily accessible place in your home with the succinct, but attention-grabbing title of "*If I Die*."

We have included a form on the next page that you can use as a basis for information to be included in the file.

If I Die

the following information will help settle my Estate:

INFORMATION FOR DEATH CERTIFICATE

MY FULL LEGAL NAME _____

MY SOCIAL SECURITY NO. _____

BIRTH DATE AND BIRTH PLACE _____

If naturalized, date & place _____

MY FATHER'S NAME _____

MY MOTHER'S MAIDEN NAME _____

PEOPLE TO BE NOTIFIED

_____

_____

_____

FUNERAL AND BURIAL ARRANGEMENTS

LOCATION OF BURIAL SITE

_____

LOCATION OF PRENEED FUNERAL CONTRACT

_____

FOR VETERAN or SPOUSE BURIAL IN A NATIONAL CEMETERY

BRANCH_____SERIAL NO._____

VETERAN'S RANK _____

VETERAN'S VA CLAIM NUMBER _____

DATE AND PLACE OF ENTRY INTO SERVICE:

_____

DATE AND PLACE OF SEPARATION FROM SERVICE:

_____

LOCATION OF OFFICIAL MILITARY DISCHARGE

OR DD 214 FORM_____

LOCATION OF LEGAL DOCUMENTS

BIRTH CERTIFICATE _____

MARRIAGE CERTIFICATE_____

PREMARITAL/MARITAL AGREEMENT_____

DIVORCE DECREE _____

PASSPORT _____

WILL OR TRUST _____

DEEDS _____

MORTGAGES _____

TITLE TO MOTOR VEHICLES _____

POWER OF ATTORNEY _____

LIVING WILL _____

Attorney name & telephone _____

LOCATION OF FINANCIAL RECORDS

INSURANCE POLICIES:
Name of Company, Location of Policy, Insurance Agent

_____

PENSIONS/ANNUITIES:
IF FEDERAL RETIREE: PIN NUMBER: _____

NAME OF SURVIVOR _____

SURVIVOR PIN NUMBER _____

BANK
Name and address of Bank, Account Number,
Location of Safe Deposit Box and Key

_____

_____

SECURITIES
Broker name and telephone number

_____

TAX RECORDS FOR PAST THREE YEARS
LOCATION _____

Accountant name and telephone number

_____

KEEPING UP TO DATE

We discussed people's natural disinclination to make an Estate Plan until they are faced with their own mortality. Many believe that they will make just one Will and then die (maybe that's why they put off making a Will). The reality is, most people who make a Will change it at least once before they die. If you have an Estate Plan, it is important to update it when any of the following events take place:

✍ CHANGE IN MARITAL STATUS
GETTING MARRIED

In the early 20th century, marriage was a simple thing. Two young people fell in love, and married. There was no need for an Antenuptial (i.e., Premarital) Agreement because they came to the marriage with little property and an intent to stay together "till death do us part." Today, young people tend to postpone marriage until they have established careers, so they are coming into the marriage with property they worked hard to acquire. The intent to remain married remains, but young people are realistic. They know the statistics. Half of the marriages don't work out. But, ever optimistic, the majority of those who divorce will marry at least once again, and in many cases, with children from a prior union.

It is a foolhardy couple who enter a marriage in today's society without an Antenuptial Agreement that spells out the rights and responsibilities of the couple in the event that one of them dies, or they divorce. Courts in Ohio will enforce the agreement, provided the document was signed voluntarily, after full disclosure of the finances of each party (*Fletcher v. Fletcher*, 628 N.E.2 1343 (Ohio, 1994)). A document that is too one-sided can be challenged in Court, so it is important that each parties be represented by his own attorney.

Once the honeymoon is over, it is important to examine your pre-marriage Estate Plan. As explained in Chapter 5, if you do not change the Will you signed before you married, your spouse may be able to challenge that Will, unless your Antenuptial Agreement gives up marital rights.

You should review your Antenuptial Agreement on a regular basis as your finances change or as you have children. With the consent of your spouse, you can amend your Agreement. If it needs a complete revision, you can revoke the agreement, and replace it with a Marital Agreement. Changes to the original Agreement need to be prepared and signed in the same manner as your original agreement. There needs to be full disclosure by both parties as to the extent of their wealth. Again, each party should be represented by his own attorney.

GETTING DIVORCED

Under Ohio law, should you divorce and then die before you get around to changing your Will, any gift that you made in your Will or Trust for your former spouse is revoked. Your Probate Estate will be distributed as if your spouse died before you did (ORC 2107.33). Unless the divorce decree states otherwise, personal property owned jointly with right of survivorship becomes an interest in common, with each partner owning a share of the property in proportion to his net contribution (ORC 5815.34). But it is best not to rely on the law. If you own a bank account jointly with your spouse, there might be considerable disagreement about how much you contributed to the account. And the statute makes no mention of what happens to real property you own. If you own real property with right of survivor, that right might continue unless your divorce decree states otherwise, or you and your former spouse agree to change it to a Tenancy In Common.

If you divorce (or even separate) it is important to review all of your Estate Planning documents (deeds, pension plans, insurance policies, Will or Trust etc.) to determine whether you wish to name a new beneficiary.

✍ A CHANGE IN RELATIONSHIP

If you marry, separate, divorce, have a child, or if a beneficiary of your Estate dies, you need to examine your Will to determine whether it needs to be revised. It is important to have changes made by a properly drafted and signed document. If you make changes by crossing things out or writing over your Will, the validity of the document can be challenged once you die.

Simply ripping up the old Will effectively revokes the Will (ORC 2107.33). But it could happen that someone (perhaps your attorney) has a copy of the Will. If no one knows that you revoked the Will, they may think the Will is lost and offer a copy of the Will for Probate (see page 90). Best to have a new Will prepared with the opening paragraph stating "I hereby revoke all prior Wills."

NOTIFY EMPLOYER OF CHANGE

If you change your marital status (either marry or divorce) you need to tell your employer of the change so that the employer can change your status for purposes of paycheck tax deductions. A health insurance or pension plan that provides benefits for a spouse, needs to be changed as well. As explained in Chapter 6, Ohio law allows an employer to give up to $2,500 of the decedent's final wages to a member of his immediate family (spouse, adult child, parent) in that order (ORC 2113.04). If you change your marital status, you need to inform your employer, in writing, who is to receive your unpaid wages in the event of your death. Ask your employer to put that writing in your work file.

BENEFICIARY MOVES OR DIES

Most people remember to name an alternate beneficiary should one of their beneficiaries die. But how many of us remember to notify the pension plan or insurance company when a beneficiary moves? Many life insurance proceeds are never paid because the company cannot locate the beneficiary. The Actuarial Office of the Federal Employees' Group Life Insurance Program reported that as of September, 2003, they had over 55.8 million dollars in unpaid benefits, mostly because they could not locate the beneficiary at the last given address.

EXECUTOR MOVES OR DIES

If you filed your Will with the Court, the Clerk placed it in a wrapper identifying the name and address of the person to whom it is to be delivered in the event of your death (ORC 2107.07). In most cases, that person will be the Executor named in your Will. If your Executor moves, you need to inform the Clerk of the change of address.

If your Executor moves out of state, consider appointing another who is a resident of Ohio. The Court will not appoint an out of state Personal Representative unless that person is related to you through blood or marriage, or unless the state your Executor lives in allows the appointment of a non-resident Personal Representative (ORC 2109.21). But even if your Executor qualifies as an out of state Personal Representative, it will be more convenient, and perhaps less expensive, to have someone who lives in Ohio serve as you Personal Representative.

If your Executor dies before you do, you may need to change your Will and name another person for the job. The revised Will needs to be deposited with the Clerk, along with a new wrapper giving the name and address of the new Executor.

✍ RELOCATION TO A NEW STATE OR COUNTRY

There is no need to change your Estate Plan for a move within the state of Ohio. If your attorney has your original Will, or any other of your original documents, then unless you intend to continue to employ him as your attorney, you need to retrieve your originals and take them with you to the new state.

If you deposited your Will with the Probate Court, you need to retrieve your Will and then deposit it in the Probate Court of the county of your new residence. If you are moving out of state, you need to take the Will with you. Not all states allow a Will to be deposited with the Court prior to the death of the Will maker. You may need to make other arrangements for the storage of your Will in the new state.

You need to determine whether your Will conforms to the laws of the state of your new residence. Most states will honor a Will drafted according to Ohio law, however, the rights of a spouse vary considerably state to state. If you are married and have not provided the minimum amount as required by the laws of the new state, should you die before your spouse, your Will may be challenged on that basis. The same applies to a Trust. Most states allow a surviving spouse to demand funds from the Trust of the decedent spouse, if the deceased spouse did not provide the minimum amount to his spouse as required by the laws of that state.

If you do not have a Will, it is important to check out the Laws of Descent and Distribution for that state. In some states they are called in Laws of Intestate Succession. Each state has its own laws of inheritance of property and those laws are very different from each other.

Who has the right to inherit your property in the state of Ohio may be different from who can inherit your property in another state. If you do not have a Will, this is the time to think about who will inherit your property should you die in the state of your new residence.

This is especially important for those who are married. The right of a spouse to inherit property varies significantly from state to state. There is a world of difference in the rights of a spouse in a Community Property state (Arizona, California, Idaho, Louisiana, Nevada, New Mexico, Texas, Washington and Wisconsin) and other states. There is even variation in the rights of a spouse from one Community Property state to another!

OTHER ESTATE PLANNING DOCUMENTS

A *Medical* or *Health Care Directive* is a document that gives instructions about the health care a person does (or does not) want to receive in the event that he is too ill to make his own health care decisions. In Ohio, that document is called a *Durable Power of Attorney For Health Care* with your *Attorney In Fact* given authority to make medical decisions (ORC 1337.13).

If you have a Ohio Durable Power of Attorney for Health Care, it is best to sign a new Health Care Directive should you move to another state. Other states have laws that enable you to appoint someone with powers similar to your Attorney In Fact, but the laws of the state may refer to such person as a *Patient Advocate* or a *Health Care Surrogate* or a *Health Care Agent*. It is best to have a Health Care Directive using the forms and terms that are recognized in that state, rather than chance any confusion should you become ill and find yourself in an emergency situation.

Similarly, if you appointed someone to handle your finances under a Power of Attorney, you may want to have another prepared in conformity with the laws of the new state, so there will be no question of the right of your Attorney In Fact to conduct business on your behalf.

TAX CONCERNS

You also need to check out the taxes of the new state. Each state has its own tax structure. Some states have an inheritance tax, or a transfer tax on all inherited property. If state taxes are high, you may need an Estate Plan that will minimize the impact of those taxes.

CREDITOR PROTECTION

Creditor protection is another thing that is significantly different state to state. If you have much debt, then determine what items can be inherited by your family free of your debts.

When moving to another state you need to either educate yourself about the laws of the state, or consult with an attorney who can assist you in reviewing your Estate Plan to see if that plan will accomplish your goals in that state.

CHANGE OF FORTUNE

Most of us do not have the good fortune of winning a lottery, nor the bad fortune of going bankrupt. However, we all have our ups and downs. It is important to review your finances every now and again to determine exactly what it is that you will be leaving to your beneficiaries. If you have included a cash gift to a beneficiary, you need to be sure that your Probate Estate has enough money to make the gift. Accounts that you own jointly, or hold in a Pay On Death or In Trust For account, will bypass Probate and be given directly to the beneficiary.

You cannot include such accounts as part of your Will or Trust because you have already made a gift of those funds. If you wish to change the amount or the beneficiary of those accounts, you will need to do so during your lifetime.

✍ A SIGNIFICANT CHANGE IN THE LAW

A major problem associated with the legal system in the United States is its volatility. Changes might be easy to keep up with if we had only one set of laws. But we are ruled by federal statutes and regulations and state statutes and regulations. We pay state and federal legislators to make laws and change existing statutes and regulations. We pay judges to tell us the meaning of the law, but their interpretation of the law may change the way the law operates. The legislature and the judiciary do their job and so laws and regulations change frequently and often without prior notice.

We, the public, are charged with the duty of understanding the law. Many a citizen has been chided with "Ignorance of the law is no excuse." Most of us have a general concept of what is, and what is not, allowed in our society, however, when presented with a particular problem, we may need to turn to a professional (lawyer, accountant, journalist, city official, etc.) to get an explanation of the law.

Areas of the law that affect you and your family, personally, are discussed in this book, namely Probate Law, Tax Law, and Estate Planning (Wills and Trusts). It is important to keep up with news in these areas to learn about changes in the law that may affect your Estate Plan. It is a good idea to check with your attorney on a regular basis to determine whether you need to change your Will or Trust because of a change in state or federal law.

Also check out the Eagle Publishing Company Web site for changes we will post to keep this book fresh.
http://www.eaglepublishing.com

GAMES DECEDENTS PLAY

We discussed the game of "hide and seek" some decedents play with their heirs. A variation of that game is the "wild goose chase." The person who plays this game is one who never updates his files. His records are filled with all sorts of lapsed insurance policies, promissory notes of debts long since paid; brokerage statements of securities that have been sold, and so on.

When he is gone, his family will become frustrated as they try to hunt down the "missing" asset. If you wish to play this game, then the best joke is to keep the key to a safe deposit box that you are no longer leasing. That will keep folks hunting for a long time!

If you do not have a wicked sense of humor, then do your family a favor and update your records on a regular basis.

Glossary

ABSTRACT OF TITLE An *Abstract of Title* is a condensed history of the title to real property. It consists of a summary of all the recorded documents, including mortgages, that affect title to a given parcel of land.

ADMINISTRATION The *Administration* of a Probate Estate is the management and settlement of the decedent's affairs. There are different types of administration. See *Ancillary Administration.*

ADMINISTRATIVE LAW JUDGE An *Administrative Law Judge* is someone who is appointed to conduct an administrative hearing. He has the power to administer oaths, take testimony, and then decide the facts of the case. Although he can decide the facts of the case, the final outcome of the hearing is decided by the government agency that appointed the Administrative Law Judge.

AFFIANT An *Affiant* is someone who signs an affidavit and swears or acknowledges that it is true in the presence of a notary public or other person with authority to administer an oath or take acknowledgments.

AFFIDAVIT An *Affidavit* is a written statement of fact made by someone voluntarily, under oath, or acknowledged as being true, in the presence of a notary public or someone else who has authority to administer an oath or take acknowledgments.

AGENT An *Agent* is someone who is authorized by another (the *principal)* to act for, or in place, of the principal.

ANATOMICAL GIFT   An *Anatomical Gift* is the donation of all or part of the body of the decedent for the purpose of transplantation or research.

ANCILLARY ADMINISTRATION An *Ancillary Administration* is a Probate proceeding that aids or assists the original (primary) Probate proceeding. Ancillary administration is conducted to determine the beneficiary of the decedent's property located within that state, and to determine whether the property is taxable in that state.

ANNUAL GIFT TAX EXCLUSION The *Annual Gift Tax Exclusion* is the amount a person can gift to another each year without being required to file a federal Gift Tax Return. For the year 2006, the Annual Gift Tax Exclusion is equal to $12,000.

ANNUITANT An *Annuitant* is someone who is entitled to receive payments under an Annuity contract.

ANNUITY An *Annuity* is a contract that gives someone (the Annuitant) the right to receive periodic payments (monthly, quarterly) for the life of the Annuitant or for a given number of years.

ANTENUPTIAL AGREEMENT An *Antenuptial Agreement* (also known as a *Prenuptial* or *Premarital Agreement*) is an agreement made prior to marriage whereby a couple provides for the management of the property during marriage and how their property is to be divided should one die, or they later divorce.

ASSET An *asset* is anything owned by someone that has a value, including personal property (jewelry, paintings, securities, cash, motor vehicles, etc.) and real property (condominiums, vacant lots, acreage, residences, etc.).

ASSIGN To *assign* is to transfer one's rights in or to something to another. For example, a contract may allow a party to assign his rights in the contract to another person.

ATTORNEY or ATTORNEY AT LAW An *attorney*, also known as an *Attorney at law*, or a *lawyer*, is someone who is licensed by the state to practice law in that state.

ATTORNEY IN FACT An *Attorney In Fact* is someone appointed to act as an Agent for another (the Principal) under a Power of Attorney.

BASIS The *basis* is a value that is assigned to an asset for the purpose of determining the gain (or loss) on the sale of the item or in determining the value of the item in the hands of someone who has received it as a gift.

BENEFICIARY A *beneficiary* is one who benefits from the act of another or from the transfer of property. In this book we refer to a beneficiary as someone named in a Will, Trust, or deed to receive property, or someone who inherits property under the Laws of Intestate Succession.

BOND A *bond* required by the Probate Court is a written document that guarantees the Personal Representative will perform his duties as required by law. The person or company that insures the performance of the Personal Representative is called a *surety.* The value of the bond is set by the Court. The cost of purchasing the bond is charged to the decedent's Estate.

CAPITAL GAINS TAX A *Capital Gains Tax* is a tax on the amount the net sales proceeds exceeds the basis of a capital asset sold by a taxpayer.

CAVEAT *Caveat* is Latin for "Let him beware." It is a warning for the reader to be careful.

CERTIFICATE OF TITLE A *Certificate of Title* is a document that is recorded by the Clerk in the Court of Common Pleas in the county where the property is located. The Certificate identifies the legal description of the property and the identity of the current owner.

CFR   *CFR* is the abbreviation for the *Code of Federal Regulations.*

CLAIM A *claim* against the decedent's Estate is a demand for payment of a debt of the decedent. To be effective, the claim must be filed with the Probate Court within the time limits set by law.

CODE A *Code* is a body of laws arranged systematically for easy reference e.g. the Internal Revenue Code.

COLUMBARIUM A *Columbarium* is a separate room or building with niches (spaces) designed to store urns containing the ashes of cremated bodies.

COMMISSION A *commission* is compensation paid to someone for performing a service. In Ohio, commission paid to the Personal Representative is calculated as a percentage of Estate property (ORC 2113.35).

COMMISSIONER A *Commissioner* is someone appointed by the Court or by the government to do a job.

COMMON LAW MARRIAGE A *Common Law marriage* is one that is entered into without a state marriage license or any kind of official marriage ceremony. A Common Law marriage is created by an agreement to marry, followed by the two living together, and telling everyone they know that they are husband and wife. Ohio does not recognize a Common Law marriage unless it was entered into in this state before October 10, 1991 (ORC 3105.12)

COMMUNITY PROPERTY Certain states (Arizona, California, Idaho, Louisiana, Nevada, New Mexico, Texas, Washington, and Wisconsin) have laws stating that property acquired by husband or wife, or both, during their marriage is *Community Property* and is owned equally by both of them.

CONTINGENT BENEFICIARY A *Contingent Beneficiary* is an alternate beneficiary; i.e. someone who inherits if the primary beneficiary dies or loses the right to inherit.

CONFLICT OF INTEREST A *conflict of interest* is a conflict between the official duties of a fiduciary (Guardian, Trustee, attorney, etc.) and his own private interest. For example, it is a conflict of interest for a Successor Trustee to use Trust property for his own personal profit.

COURT The *Court* as used in this book is the Probate Court. When referring to an order made by the court, the term is synonymous with "judge," i.e., an "order of the court" is an order made by the judge of the court.

CREDITOR A *creditor* is someone to whom a debt is owed by another person (the *debtor*).

CREMAINS *Cremains* is shorthand for *cremated remains*. It refers to the ashes of a person who was cremated.

CURTESY *Curtesy* is the right of a husband, upon the death of his wife, to a life estate in real property she owned during their marriage, provided they had a surviving child who could inherit the property. This English Common Law was abolished in Ohio, however, Dower rights were extended to both husband and wife.

CUSTODIAN A *Custodian* under Ohio's ***Transfers to Minors Act*** is a person or a financial institution that accepts responsibility for the care and management of property given to a minor child, until the child is an adult.

DAMAGES *Damages* is money that is awarded by a Court as compensation to someone who has been injured by the action of another.

DEBTOR A *debtor* is someone who owes payment of money or services to another person (the *creditor*).

DECEDENT The *Decedent* is the person who died.

DECLARATORY JUDGMENT A ***Declaratory Judgment*** is a determination of the parties rights and status, even though no one is awarded damages (i.e., compensation).

DEED OF TRUST A ***Deed of Trust*** is a deed that places title to real property in Trust to secure payment of monies owed on the property. It serves the same function as a mortgage.

DESCENDANT A *descendant* is someone who descends from a common ancestor. There are two kinds of descendants: a *lineal descendant* and a *collateral descendant*. The lineal descendant is one who descends in a straight line such as father to son to grandson. The collateral descendant is one who descends in a parallel line, such as a cousin. In this book, unless otherwise stated, the term *descendant* refers to a *lineal descendant*.

DISTRIBUTION The *distribution* of a Trust or Probate Estate is the giving to the beneficiary that part of the Estate to which the beneficiary is entitled.

DOMESTIC PARTNER A ***Domestic Partner*** is a relationship established by the California legislature. California statute gives a same gender couple, and heterosexual couples over the age of 62, the right to become Domestic Partners by filling out a Declaration of Domestic Partner with the California Secretary of State. Registered Domestic Partners.

DOWER In Ohio, ***Dower*** is the right of a husband or wife to a Life Estate in one-third of all real property owned by the spouse during their marriage.

DURABLE POWER OF ATTORNEY A ***Durable Power of Attorney*** is a document in which the person who signs the document (the *Principal*) gives another person (his *Attorney in Fact*) authority to do certain things on behalf of the Principal. The Attorney in Fact is also referred to as the Principal's *Agent*. The word *"durable"* means that the authority of the Agent continues even if the Principal is incapacitated at the time that the Agent is acting on behalf of the Principal.

DURABLE POWER OF ATTORNEY FOR HEALTH CARE A ***Durable Power of Attorney for Health Care*** is a Health Care Directive that gives the Attorney In Fact authority to make medical decisions for the Principal in the event that the Principal is too ill to make decisions for himself.

ELECTIVE SHARE The ***Elective Share*** is the minimum amount of the decedent's estate that a surviving spouse is entitled to receive under the law. In Ohio, if the decedent's Will does not provide for this minimum value, the surviving spouse can elect to take the amount (s)he would have received had the decedent died without a Will.

ENCUMBRANCE   An *encumbrance* is a claim or a lien or a liability that is attached to real property, such as a mortgage, or lease or a mechanic's lien.

EQUITABLE *Equitable* is whatever is right or just. If property is distributed to two or more people equitably, then the division is not necessarily equal, but according to the principles of justice or fairness.

EQUITY The *equity* in a home is the market value of the home less monies owed on the property (mortgages, tax liens, etc.)

ESTATE A person's *Estate* is all of the property (both real and personal property) owned by that person. The decedent's Estate may also be referred to as his *Taxable Estate* because all of the decedent's assets must be included when determining whether Estate Taxes are due. Compare to PROBATE ESTATE.

EXECUTOR An *Executor* (feminine *Executrix*) is a legal term found in many Wills. The terms refer to the person appointed by the Will maker to carry out directions given in the Will. In modern Wills, this term has been replaced by *Personal Representative.*

FAIR MARKET VALUE The *Fair Market Value* of a home is the amount at which the property would change hands between a willing buyer and seller, both having reasonable knowledge of the facts.

FIDUCIARY A *Fiduciary* is one who takes on the duty of holding property in Trust for another or acting for the benefit of another, such as a Personal Representative, Trustee, Guardian etc.. A fiduciary relationship is also one that is developed out of trust and confidence. For example, an attorney has a fiduciary relationship with his client.

FRATERNAL BENEFIT SOCIETY A *Fraternal Benefit Society* is a not-for-profit society or voluntary association that is organized to accomplish some worthy civic goal, and for the mutual benefit of its members.

GRANTEE   The *Grantee* of a deed is the person who receives title to real property from the *Grantor*.

GRANTOR   The *Grantor* is someone who transfers property. The Grantor of a deed is the person who transfers real property to a new owner (the Grantee). The Grantor of a Trust is someone who creates the Trust and then transfers property into the Trust. Also see SETTLOR.

GUARANTOR A *Guarantor* is someone who promises to pay a debt or perform a contract for another person in the event that person does not fulfill his obligation.

GUARDIAN A *Guardian* is someone who has legal authority to care for the person and/or property of a minor or someone who has been found by the Court to be incapacitated.

HEALTH CARE DIRECTIVE A *Health Care Directive* is a statement made by someone (the *principal)* in the presence of witnesses or a written, notarized statement in which the principal gives directions about the care he wishes to receive. See DURABLE POWER OF ATTORNEY FOR HEALTH CARE and LIVING WILL.

HOMESTEAD The *homestead* is the dwelling and land owned and occupied as the owner's principal residence.

HEIR   An *heir* is anyone entitled to inherit the decedent's property under the Laws of Descent and Distribution in the event that the decedent dies without a Will.

INCAPACITATED   The term *incapacitated* is used in two ways: a person is *physically incapacitated* if he has a physical disability. A person is *legally incapacitated* if a Court finds that a person is unable to care for his person or property. Once a judge determines that a person is legally incapacitated, he will appoint someone to care for the person and/or property of the incapacitated person.

INDIGENT   A person who is *indigent* is one who is poor and without funds.

IRA ACCOUNT   An *Individual Retirement Account ("IRA")* is a retirement savings account in which income taxes on certain deposits and interest to the account are deferred until the monies are withdrawn.

IRREVOCABLE TRUST   An *Irrevocable Trust* is a Trust that cannot be changed, cancelled or terminated until its purpose is accomplished.

INSOLVENT   A person or business is *insolvent* if more money is owed than owned, or if the person or business is unable to pay debts as they come due.

INTER VIVOS TRUST   An *Inter Vivos Trust* (also known as a *Living Trust*) is a Trust that is created and becomes effective during the lifetime of the Grantor (or Settlor) as opposed to a Trust that he includes as part of his Will to take effect upon his death.

INTESTATE   *Intestate* means not having a Will or dying without a Will. *Testate* is to have a Will or dying with a Will.

JOINT AND SEVERAL LIABILITY If two or more people agree to be *jointly and severally liable* to pay a debt, then each individually agrees to be responsible to pay the debt, and together they all agree to pay for the debt.

JOINT TENANCY In Ohio, a *Joint Tenancy* means that each tenant owns an equal share of the property. There is no right of survivorship unless the deed specifically says so.

KEY MAN INSURANCE *Key man insurance* is an insurance policy designed to protect a company from economic loss in the event that an important employee of the company becomes disabled or dies.

KEOGH PLAN A *Keogh Plan* is a retirement plan available to self-employed taxpayers. Certain tax benefits are available such as tax deductions for annual contributions to the plan. The plan is named for its author, Eugene James Keogh.

LAWS OF DESCENT AND DISTRIBUTION *The Laws of Descent and Distribution* are the laws of the state relating to who is entitled to inherit the decedent's Probate Estate when he dies without a valid Will. These laws are also called the *Laws of Intestate Succession.*

LEGALESE *Legalese* refers to the use of legal terms and confusing text that is used by some attorneys to draft legal documents.

LETTERS *Letters* is a document, issued by the Probate court, giving the Personal Representative authority to take possession of and to administer the decedent's Estate.

LIEN A *lien* is a charge against a person's property as security for a debt. The lien is evidence of the creditor's right to take the property as full or partial payment, in the event that the debtor defaults in paying the monies owed.

LIFE ESTATE A *Life Estate* interest in real property is the right to possess and occupy the property for so long as the owner of the Life Estate lives. When the owner of the Life Estate dies, the property will belong to the owner of the *Remainder Interest*.

LITIGATION *Litigation* is the process of carrying on a lawsuit, i.e., to sue for some right or remedy in a court of law. A Litigation Attorney is one who is experienced in conducting the law suit and in particular, going to trial.

LIVING WILL A *Living Will* is a Health Care Directive that gives instructions about whether life support systems should be withheld or withdrawn in the event that the person who signs the Living Will is terminally ill or in a persistent vegetative state and unable to speak for himself.

MEDICAID *Medicaid* is a public assistance program sponsored jointly by the federal and state government to provide Medical Assistance for people with low income and limited assets.

MOBILE OR MANUFACTURED HOME A *mobile* or *manufactured home* is a structure that is built on a permanent chassis (i.e. supporting frame). It is transportable in one or more sections. It is designed for use as a dwelling with provision made for connection to utilities.

NET PROCEEDS The *net proceeds* of a sale is the sale price less costs and expenses paid to make the sale.

Guiding Those Left Behind In Ohio

NET PROBATE ESTATE The *Net Probate Estate* is the value of the decedent Probate Estate, less all the monies paid to settle the Estate, i.e. what is left once all valid claims and the costs and expenses of the Probate procedure are paid.

NET WORTH A person's *net worth* is the value of all of the property that he owns less the monies he owes.

NEXT OF KIN *Next of kin* has two meanings in law: *next of kin* refers to a person's nearest blood relation or it can refer to those people (not necessarily blood relations) who are entitled to inherit the property of a person who dies without a valid Will.

NON-PROBATE TRANSFER A *non-Probate Transfer* is the transfer of property to the decedent's beneficiary without the necessity of a Probate Procedure. This includes property that is transferred to the surviving joint owner, or property transferred to the beneficiary of a Pay On Death accounts.

ORC *ORC* is the abbreviation used in this book for the OHIO REVISED CODE.

PERJURY *Perjury* is lying under oath. The false statement can be made as a witness in court or by signing an Affidavit. Perjury is a criminal offense.

PERSONAL EFFECTS *Personal effects* is personal property that is kept for one's personal use such as clothing, jewelry, books, and other items generally found in the home.

PERSONAL PROPERTY *Personal property* is all property owned by a person that is not real property (real estate). It includes personal effects, cars, securities, bank accounts, insurance policies, etc.

PERSONAL REPRESENTATIVE A *Personal Representative* is someone appointed by the Probate Court to settle the decedent's Estate and to distribute whatever is left to the proper beneficiary.

PER STIRPES *Per Stirpes* is a method of distributing property to a group of beneficiaries. In the event a beneficiary dies before the gift is distributed, the deceased person's share goes to his descendants. If he has no descendants, the surviving beneficiaries share equally in the gift.

PETITION A *Petition* is a formal written, request to a Court asking the Court to take action or issue an order on a given matter; e.g. a request to appoint a Guardian.

POSTNUPTIAL AGREEMENT A *Postnuptial Agreement* is an agreement made by a couple after marriage to decide their respective rights in case of a dissolution or the death of a spouse.

POWER OF ATTORNEY A *Power of Attorney* is a document in which someone (the *Principal*) gives another person (his *Agent* or *Attorney In Fact*) authority to do certain things on behalf of the Principal.

PRINCIPAL The *Principal* of a Power of Attorney is the person who permits or directs another (his *Attorney-In-Fact* or *Agent*) to act for him.

PROBATE *Probate* is a Court procedure in which a Court determines the existence of a valid Will. The decedent's Estate is then settled by the Personal Representative who pays all valid claims and then distributes whatever remains to the proper beneficiary.

PROBATE ESTATE The *Probate Estate* is that part of the decedent's Estate that is subject to Probate. It includes property that the decedent owned in his name only or as a Tenant In Common. It does not include property that was owned jointly with right of survivorship, or in trust for another.

PRO BONO The term *Pro Bono* means "for the public good." When an attorney works Pro Bono, he does so voluntarily and without pay.

PUNITIVE DAMAGES *Punitive damages* are awarded by a Court to punish someone who deliberately disregarded the rights or safety of another. It is money awarded in addition to *compensatory damages* which are monies awarded to reimburse the wronged person for actual losses.

QRP *QRP* is the abbreviation for a *Qualified Retirement Plan.* It is a retirement plan that qualifies for certain federal income tax deferrals or credits.

REAL PROPERTY *Real property,* also known as *real estate,* is land and anything permanently attached to the land such as buildings and fences.

REMAINDER INTEREST The *Remainder Interest* in real property is the property that passes to the owner of that Interest, once the owner of the Life Estate dies. See LIFE ESTATE

RESIDUARY BENEFICIARY A *Residuary Beneficiary* of a Will is a beneficiary who is entitled to whatever is left of the Probate Estate once specific gifts made in the Will have been distributed and the decedent's bills, taxes and costs of Probate have been paid.

RESIDUARY ESTATE The *Residuary Estate* is that part of the Probate Estate that is left after all the debts, taxes, and costs of administration are paid and specific gifts distributed.

REVOCABLE TRUST   A *Revocable Trust* is a Trust which can be amended or revoked by the Settlor during his lifetime.

REVOCABLE LIVING TRUST A *Revocable Living Trust* (also known as an *Inter Vivos Trust*) is a Revocable Trust that is created and becomes effective during the lifetime of the Settlor.

RIGHT OF SURVIVORSHIP A *Right of Survivorship* is the right of the survivor of a deceased person to the property of the decedent.

SECURED DEBT A *secured debt* is a debt backed by property. If the borrower does not pay the loan, the lender can take the property. Car loans and mortgages are secured debts.

SETTLOR A *Settlor* Is someone who creates and then funds a Trust.

SIBLING   A *sibling* is one of two or more people born of the same parents; i.e., a brother or a sister. Unless, otherwise noted, we used the term to include those who have only one parent in common; i.e. a half brother or a half sister.

SOLEMNIZE   To *solemnize* a marriage is to enter a marriage publicly, before witnesses, rather than privately as in a common law marriage.

SPECIFIC GIFT A *Specific Gift* is a gift of a specific item, or part of the Will maker's Estate, that is made to a named beneficiary of the Will.

SPENDTHRIFT A *spendthrift* is someone who spends money carelessly or wastefully or extravagantly.

SPENDTHRIFT TRUST A *Spendthrift Trust* is a Trust created to provide monies to a beneficiary, and at the same time protect the Trust property from being taken by the creditors of the beneficiary.

SSI *SSI* Is the abbreviation for *Supplemental Security Income*, a federal benefit given to qualified disabled persons

STATUTE OF LIMITATION A *Statute of Limitation* is a federal or state law that sets maximum time periods for taking legal action. Once the time set out in the statute passes, no legal action can be taken.

STATUTORY AGENT A *Statutory Agent* of a corporation is someone who is authorized to act on behalf of the company and accept service of process in the event the company is sued.

STEPPED-UP BASIS A *stepped-up basis* is the fair market value placed on property that is purchased or inherited from another. The "step-up" refers to the increase in value from the basis of the former owner (usually what he paid for it), to the basis of the new owner (usually the market value when the transfer is made).

SUCCESSOR TRUSTEE A *Successor Trustee* is someone who takes the place of the Trustee.

SUPPORT ALLOWANCE The *Support Allowance* is the amount set aside from the decedent's creditor claims for the support and maintenance of the surviving spouse and minor children. In Ohio, that amount is $40,000.

SURVIVORSHIP DEED A *Survivorship Deed* is a deed that places title to real property in the name of two or more joint owners such that should one of them die, the survivor(s) continue to own the property as joint tenants with right of survivorship.

TENANCY BY THE ENTIRETY A *Tenancy by the Entirety* is a form of ownership of real property held by a husband and wife. It is a joint tenancy with right of survivorship, modified by the Common Law concept that the husband and wife are one. This means that each owns 100% of the property both before and after death. A creditor of one of the partners may not enforce a lien against property owned by them as Tenants by the Entirety, because the other partner owns the property 100%. After April 4, 1985, property in Ohio may be conveyed to a married couple as a Survivorship Tenancy and not as Tenants by the Entirety. With a Survivorship Tenancy, each owns an equal share of the property until death, when the surviving owner owns it 100%. A creditor of one of the partners may enforce a lien against the Survivorship property. Once he does so, the property becomes a Tenancy in Common, with the creditor having access to the debtors share of the property (ORC 5302.20).

TENANCY IN COMMON *Tenancy In Common* is a form of ownership such that each Tenant owns his share without any claim to that share by the other owners. There is no right of survivorship. Should a Tenant In Common die, his share belongs to his Estate and not to the surviving owners.

TESTATE *Testate* means having made a Will or dying with a Will.

TESTATOR A *Testator* (feminine *Testatrix*) is someone who makes and signs a Will; or someone who dies leaving a Will.

TITLE INSURANCE *Title Insurance* is a policy issued by a title insurance company after searching title to the property. The insurance covers losses that result from a defect of title, such as unpaid taxes, or a claim of ownership of the property.

TORRENS TITLE SYSTEM The *Torrens Title System* (named for Sir Richard Torrens) is a system for registering title to land by applying to the Court to determine the owner of the property and then issue a Certificate of Title.

TRUST AGREEMENT A *Trust Agreement* is a document in which someone (the Settlor or Trustor) creates a Trust and appoints a Trustee to manage property placed into the Trust. The usual purpose of the Trust is to benefit persons or organizations named by the Settlor as beneficiaries of the Trust.

TRUSTEE A *Trustee* is a person, or institution, who accepts the duty of managing Trust property for the benefit of another.

TRUSTOR A *Trustor* is someone who creates a Trust.

UNDUE INFLUENCE *Undue influence* is pressure, influence or persuasion that overpowers a person's free will or judgment, so that a person acts according to the will or purpose of the dominating party.

UNSECURED CREDITOR An *unsecured creditor* is someone who is owed money on a promissory note with nothing to back it up if payment is not made. A *secured creditor* holds some special assurance of payment, such as a mortgage on real property or a lien on a car.

VOID GIFT A *void gift* is one that is not legally enforceable. For example, if a Will makes a gift and the Court finds that provision to be void, the beneficiary has no legal right to receive that gift.

WAIVER   A *waiver* is the intentional and voluntary giving up of a known right.

WARRANTY DEED A *Warranty Deed* is a deed in which the Grantor warrants (promises) that the property he is transferring has good and clear title; i.e., that no one else has rights in the property. This is different than a *Quit-claim Deed* where the Grantor says, in effect, "I am releasing any interest I have in this property to you, but I make no guarantees about anyone else's right to this property."

WRONGFUL DEATH   A *wrongful death* is a death that was caused by the willful or negligent act of a person or company.

INDEX

T

WEB SITES

OHIO WEB SITES

203 Ohio Statutes are referenced in
Guiding Those Left Behind In Ohio

Each state has its own set of laws relating to the settlement of a person's Estate. The laws that are referenced in this book are very different from the laws of other states.

The author is in now in the process of "translating"
Guiding Those Left Behind
for the rest of the states, that is, writing state specific books that explain how to settle the affairs of someone who dies in the given state.

Books for the following states are now in print:
ALABAMA, ARIZONA, ARKANSAS, CALIFORNIA
CONNECTICUT, FLORIDA, GEORGIA, HAWAII
ILLINOIS, INDIANA, IOWA, KANSAS
KENTUCKY, LOUISIANA, MASSACHUSETTS
MARYLAND, MICHIGAN, MINNESOTA, MISSOURI
MISSISSIPPI, NEW JERSEY, NEW YORK
NORTH CAROLINA, OHIO, OKLAHOMA
PENNSYLVANIA, SOUTH CAROLINA, TENNESSEE
TEXAS, VIRGINIA, WASHINGTON, WISCONSIN

Call EAGLE PUBLISHING COMPANY at **(800) 824-0823** to learn of the availability of books for other states.

To order books call Eagle Publishing Company or visit our Web site for a 20% discount.
http://www.eaglepublishing.com

BOOK REVIEWS OF *Guiding Those Left Behind*

ARIZONA

Ben T. Traywick of the Tombstone Epitaph said "This book is an excellent reference book that simplifies all the necessary tasks that must be done when there is a death in the family. There is even an explanation as to how you can arrange your own estate so that your heirs will not be left with a multitude of nagging problems." "The reviewer has been going through probate for two years with no end yet in sight. This book at the beginning two year ago would have helped immensely."

CALIFORNIA

Margot Petit Nichols of the Carmel Pine Cone called it a ". . .TRULY RIVETING READ." " . . . I could scarcely put it down." "This is a book that we should all have, either on our book shelves or thoughtfully placed with our important papers."

OTHER BOOKS BY AMELIA E. POHL

Beyond Grief To Acceptance and Peace

AMELIA E. POHL and the noted psychologist BARBARA J. SIMMONDS, Ph.d, have written a book for those families who have suffered a loss.

- ✧ What to say to the bereaved
- ✧ How to help a child through the loss
- ✧ Strategies to adjust to a new life-style
- ✧ When and where to seek assistance.

80 pages   6" X 9" $10 includes Shipping and Handling
TO ORDER CALL (800) 824-0823.

A Will Is Not Enough . . .

Many people who have a Will think that they have their affairs in order. They believe that their Will can take care of any problem that may arise. But the primary function of a Will is to distribute property to people named in a Will. A Will cannot:

⇨ Protect your assets and limit your debt

⇨ Provide care for a minor or disabled child

⇨ Avoid Guardianship

⇨ Appoint someone to make your health care decisions should you be unable to do so

⇨ Appoint someone to handle your finances should you be unable to do so

⇨ Arrange to pay for your health care should you need long term nursing care, including qualifying for MEDICAID.

AMELIA E. POHL, Esq. has written a series of state specific books explaining how to do all of these things. This new book series is a continuation of this book. It builds on basic Estate Planning concepts introduced in Chapter 7 of this book and then goes on to introduce other, more sophisticated, Estate Planning methods. Although the topics are sophisticated, the writing style is the same as in this book. It is written in plain English. It is intended for use by the average person.

A Will Is Not Enough is now available for:

ARIZONA, CALIFORNIA, CONNECTICUT, COLORADO
FLORIDA, GEORGIA, HAWAII, INDIANA, ILLINOIS, MARYLAND
MICHIGAN, MASSACHUSETTS, NEBRASKA, NEW JERSEY
NEW MEXICO, NEW YORK, OREGON, PENNSYLVANIA
TEXAS, VIRGINIA, WASHINGTON, WISCONSIN.

Readers of this book can purchase *A Will Is Not Enough* for $25. This includes shipping and handling. To check for book availability in other states call Eagle Publishing Company at (800) 824-0823.

How To Defend Yourself Against Your Lawyer

is a book about the unhappy experiences people have with their lawyers, beginning with that of the author AMELIA E. POHL. She became involved in a law suit and found herself in the role of client, rather than lawyer. She become concerned about lawyers who do not provide their clients with loyalty and respect. This book is a result of those concerns.

The book is divided into chapters that cover the most common problems that take people to a lawyer: divorce, probate, criminal, personal injury, starting a business, making a Will, buying a house, etc. Each chapter tells of the misadventures of the unwary as they sought the services of a lawyer without a clue as to what they were "buying." This book is funny, sad, interesting, but most of all informative. It tells the reader how to become a savvy consumer, i.e., how to find the right lawyer for the right job. If you ever find the need to employ a lawyer, you will be glad you read this book.

Copyright 2004   272 pages 6" X 9"   soft cover
$20 includes Shipping and Handling

BOOK REVIEW

TED KREITER of the SATURDAY EVENING POST said "Horror fans, forget about those tawdry tales of ghosts and vampires. Pick up Amelia E. Pohl's *How To Defend Yourself Against Your Lawyer* to read some really scary stuff. Like the story . . . of the grieving widow, Ethel, whose husband died shortly after a lawyer drafted a sweetheart will for the two of them. . . . Six months in attorney's fees later, Ethel learned that she already had her husband's money because it never needed to go through probate! . . Ethel then went out and found a good lawyer for $1,000 who was able to get her $5,000 back. You do the math. . . Following Pohl's useful advice could save a person much more than money."

It is the goal of EAGLE PUBLISHING COMPANY to keep our publications fresh.

As we receive information about changes to the federal or state law we will post an update to this edition at our Web site.

http://www.eaglepublishing.com